The New Gray's Fish Cookbook

A MENU COOKBOOK

Also by Rebecca Gray

American Artisanal:
Finding the Country's Best Real Food, from Cheese to Chocolate

Chefs Go Wild:
The Best Fish and Game Recipes on the Planet

Eat Like a Wild Man:
110 Years of Great Game and Fish Recipes

Gray's Fish Cookbook:
A Menu Cookbook

Gray's Wild Game Cookbook:
A Menu Cookbook

The New Gray's Wild Game Cookbook:
A Menu Cookbook

Venison

When Fishermen Cook Fish

As contributing editor:

Joy of Cooking:
75th Anniversary Edition

The New Gray's Fish Cookbook

A MENU COOKBOOK

Rebecca Gray

GRAYBOOKS
Lyme, New Hampshire

Text Copyright © 2009 Rebecca Gray
Illustrations Copyright © 2009 DeCourcy Taylor Jr.
All rights reserved.

ISBN-10: 0-9841471-7-9
ISBN-13: 978-0-9841471-7-5
Library of Congress Catalog Number: 2009907935

Published by
GrayBooks LLC
1 Main Street
Lyme, New Hampshire 03768
www.GrayBooksPublishers.com

First Edition
Softcover

Printed in The Unites States of America
on acid-free paper.

As before, to the kids—Hope, Caroline, Sam, Doug, and Will Gray

And now to their kids, always the most honest food critics—Madison, Timothy, Scarlett, Lila, Katie, and Jay

Contents

Acknowledgements   xv
Preface   17

Salmon 23

Whole Poached Salmon If You Must   25
    Green Mayonnaise
    Salad of Zucchini and Yellow Squash and Tomato
    Grand Marnier Rice Pudding

Salmon Scallops   29
    Watercress Salad
    Potato Gratin
    Grand Marnier Soufflé

Salmon Medallions with Black Olive and Basil Butter   32
    Fiddleheads with Fried Bread Crumbs
    Julienned Carrots
    Poached Pears and Figs
    Sugar Cookies

Grilled Whole Salmon   36
    Fresh Mozzarella Slices
    Rice Pilaf
    Peas and Artichoke Hearts
    Raspberry Tart

Salmon Hash Patties   39
    Sage Bread
    Three Green Salad

Salmon Salad   43
    Summer Popovers
    Another Grand Marnier Soufflé

Smoked Salmon Salad   46
    Fried Broccoli
    Fresh French Whole Wheat Bread
    Fruit and Cheeses

Salmon Calzone   48
    Green Salad
    Brownies

Saltwater Fish 51

Inshore Saltwater Fish 53

Grilled Bluefish   55
    Grilled Polenta
    Chicory and Escarole Salad
    Cantaloupe Ice

Bluefish Broiled with Thyme and Noisette Butter   58
    Asparagus
    Perfect Tomatoes with Cognac Dressing
    Raspberry Ice and Sugar Cookies

Broiled Striped Bass with Wild Mushrooms and Tomato   60
    Peas and Artichoke Hearts
    Chocolate Roll

Bluefish with Lime Mayonnaise   64
    Snow Peas with Peas
    Boiled New Potatoes

Broiled Weakfish with Mint and Garlic   66
    Couscous with Wild Mushrooms and Chives
    Your Nice Green Salad
    Orange Jelly

Redfish   68
    Potato Flan
    Salad of Bibb Lettuce and Bittergreens
    Chocolate Cake

Grilled Lemon-Thyme Mackerel   71
    Tomato and Eggplant Tart
    Nice Green Salad

Grilled Mackerel   74
    Pasta with Spinach and Artichoke Hearts
    Summer Popovers II
    Raspberries with Crème Anglaise

Offshore Saltwater Fish 77

Japanese Leftover Tuna	79
Sautéed Watercress	
Melon and Fortune Cookies	
Fresh Tuna Steaks	81
Pizza	
Nice Green Salad	
Blueberries with Crème Anglaise	
Grilled Tuna with Lemon Butter	84
Fried Pasta with Water Chestnuts	
Salad of Melon, Pears and Cucumbers	
Grilled Swordfish with Roasted Red Pepper Butter	87
Green and Purple Cole Slaw	
Grilled Idaho Potatoes	
Summer Trifle	
Grilled Swordfish with Garlic Butter	90
Panzanella Salad	
Strawberry Sherbet	
Grilled Swordfish Steaks	92
Corn Chowder	
Artichokes	
Apricot Ice	
Kingfish with Lime Butter	95
Banana Chips	
Tomatoes, Red and Green Peppers	
Potato Cake	
Real Tuttifrutti	
Mako Shark Steaks with Lemon Dill	98
Rice and Parsley Soup	
Green Beans with Sesame Seeds	
Sauterne	
Capered Dolphin	100
Red, Green and Yellow Pepper Salad	
Sweet Pastry with Jam	

Wahoo Steaks Shish Kebab 102
    Piña Coladas
    Banana Chips
    White Rice
    Grilled Pineapple with Orange Ice

Fish From the Tropics 105

Grilled Pompano with Mint and Orange Rind 107
    Brown Rice with Pignoli Nuts and Green Beans
    Your Nice Green Salad
    Sauterne and Sugar Cookies

Grilled Red Snapper with Lime Butter Sauce 109
    and Grilled Pineapple
    Bibb Salad
    Cornbread
    Coconut Ice Cream

Saltwater Bottom Fish 113

Chinese Grilled Flounder with Noodles 114
    Sautéed Watercress
    Pear Sorbet with Fortune Cookies

Gray Flounder 116
    Sautéed Spinach
    Fried Bread

Flounder and Scallop Soup 118
    Fried Bread
    Fig Tart

Fish Chowder 120
    Common Crackers
    Green Salad
    Gingerbread

Grilled Sea Bass with Sun-Dried Tomatoes, Pepper and Garlic 122
    Straw Potato-Corn Cake
    Your Nice Green Salad
    Honey Ice Cream

Tautog with Asparagus and Vegetables
   Your Favorite Salad
   Fried Bread
   Fresh Fruit
   Cheeses
	126

Black Sea Bass Chinese Style
   Stir-fry Snow Peas with Broccoli
   White Rice
   Fortune Cookies
	128

Shellfish 131

Oyster Stew
   Grits
   Your Own Nice Green Salad
   Apple Tart
	133

Mussels Steamed
   Grilled Lamb Chops
   Caesar Salad
   Fresh Fruit
	136

Shrimp Gratin Simple Green Salad	137
Mussel Pizza Caesar Salad	138

Little Shrimp
   Egg and Asparagus Salad
   Baked Apples
	141

Lobster with Anchovy Garlic Butter
   Tomato Bread
   Your Simplest Green Salad
   Drunk Melons
	144

Crab Cakes with Sherry and Garlic Mayonnaise Chicory Salad	146

Szechwan Crab for Sunday Night Supper
   White Rice with Soy Sauce on the Side
   Stir Fried Pea Pods
	150

Freshwater Fish 151

Stream Fish 153

Breakfast Trout Cornbread	154

Trout Fried
    Stuffed Risotto Tomatoes
    Zucchini
    Strawberry Sponge
	156

Streamside Trout with Potatoes Brownies	159

Poached Steelhead Trout with Lemon Butter Sauce
    Fava Beans with Asparagus
    Strawberries and Crème Anglaise
	160

Trout with Noisette Butter
    Sautéed Cucumbers
    Dilled New Potatoes
	163

Grilled Char with Tarragon and Shallot Butter
    Pasta with Fresh Corn and Basil
    Sautéed Cherry Tomatoes
    The Best Brownies
	165

Pan Poached Grayling
    Sautéed Potatoes with Chanterelles and Thyme
    Green Salad
    Fresh Fruit with Lightly-whipped Cream
    Almond Cookies
	167

Leftover Char Risotto
    Your Nice Green Salad
    Parmesan Rolls
    Apricot Crème Brulée
	170

Steamed Whitefish
    Squash, Broccoli, and Turnips in Wine
    Orange Oranges
	173

Walleye and Pike 175

Pike Couscous   177
    Cool Vegetables with Herb Mayonnaise
    Grilled Pineapple

Sautéed Walleye with Noisette Butter and Shallots   179
    Couscous
    Broiled Tomatoes
    Blancmange

Walleye en Papillotte   181
    Pasta with Parmesan and Romano Cheeses
    Green Salad with Oil and Vinegar
    Honeydew Ice

Walleye Steaks with Béarnaise Sauce   183
    Cabbage Patch Pasta Salad
    Apple Tart

Lemon-Lime Walleye   186
    Wild Mushroom and Potato Flan
    Salad
    Drunk Melons

Shad, Catfish, and Smelt 189

Fried Smelts with Noisette Butter   190
    Fried Parsley
    Grilled Pineapple with Strawberries

The Best Catfish   192
    Simple Green Salad
    French Bread

Fried Catfish   194
    Cole Slaw
    Grits
    Broiled Persimmons

Shad Roe   196
    Sorrel Soup
    New Boiled Potatoes
    Rhubarb Fool

Bass and Panfish 199

Almond Butter Smallmouth Bass — 201
    Chicken Consommé
    Sautéed Tomatoes
    Fried Bread
    The Pretty Easy Dessert

Little Fried Perch — 204
    Cucumber and Tomato Slices with Basil Vinaigrette
    Rosemary New Potatoes

Perch Fillets — 206
    Bay Potatoes
    Sliced Tomatoes
    Fruit

Red, White, and Green Largemouth Bass — 208
    Fried Tomato Slices
    Fried Bread
    Poached Peaches with Raspberries

Smallmouth Bass Tempura — 210
    White Rice
    Sake and Tea
    Fortune Cookies

Panfish on a Stick — 211
    Chocolate Chip Cookies

Basics 213

Index 230

Acknowledgements

As with hunting and fishing, cooking is a glorious and continuous learning process, evolving over a lifetime. For me those very first forays into the world of food prep were sparked by my mom and two of her friends, Nina Luce and Carol Farwell.

My godmother and Mom's roommate at Vassar, Nina Luce had no daughters of her own and seemed to delight in giving me birthday presents especially designed for a 1950s girl with a brain. For my sixth birthday—maybe seventh—she gave me my first cookbook, a Betty Crocker, of course. I could barely read but I could cipher out enough to make a mean brownie. Oh, I felt accomplished!

While Nina's influence was direct and specific, Carol Farwell's was by osmosis. What teenager would not be entranced with Carol's culinary ability—Le Cordon Bleu trained ability—which beguiled her many ongoing guests and made her queen of hostesses, with the very most-est indeed. Learn to cook and you're adored, she taught me by example.

And of course my mom not only identified and cherished these two great friendships, but also knew how important it was to shield me from her own parents' dire philosophy regarding food, which was that you eat only to sustain, never to enjoy. And you never cook or even talk about food—that would be disgusting. (My grandmother entered the kitchen only on cook's day off or at Christmastime to make fudge.)

So I happily acknowledge these three wonderful women for what they did—or did not—pass along when it came to my culinary development.

At the core of *The New Gray's Fish Cookbook* are the recipes and menus that Cintra Reeve and I created almost twenty-five years ago for the very first *Gray's Sporting Journal* fish cookbook. Consequently this new book—indeed much of my culinary training—is in large measure a product of Cintra's influence, her superior professional chef skills, guidance, and creativity in the kitchen. So I thank Cintra here for her long-ago help, but also for giving me a great foundation for what has become a lifelong passion for me, that of cooking and writing about food, especially all things wild.

Along with Cintra at the start of my foodie writings, there were two people in particular helped me back then and have again allowed their contributions to appear here. My thanks to Frank Foster who for years did the food photography for our magazine, *Gray's Sporting Journal*, and has allowed us to use his cover photo again for this book. Also, thank you DeCourcy "Larry" Taylor for letting us include your lovely pencil drawings again. But perhaps more importantly, Larry, you have my gratitude for imparting your beautiful sense of design and typography into everything *"Gray's"*—it still shines through today in this book.

Yet none of this would have happened without Ed who taught me how to shoot, to love the woods and wilderness, but also knew when to stop trying to teach me how to fish—for that was already deep in my soul. Ed also helped provide several of the platforms for my writings which launched me on a marvelous career of food writing—from magazines to cookbooks, a blog, and editing the wild sections of the 75th anniversary edition of the *Joy of Cooking*. It's a wonderful life and it would not have happened for me without his enthusiasm, brilliance, and vision. My best editor, best dinner guest, best mentor, best friend, best partner in all parts of an extraordinary and incredible life together—for Ed there will never be adequate acknowledgement.

Preface

In the preface for *The New Gray's Wild Game Cookbook* (GrayBooks, 2009) I wrote that revising my out-of-print game cookbook—written some twenty-five years ago and my very first book—had been sort of traumatic. In my mind I kept likening it to what I'd heard happens when a person is drowning: A whole lot of your life—the good and bad experiences—flash before your eyes making you at once grimace at your own innocence and ignorance and euphoric at the beauty of a good life. Fortunately, in the case of my cookbook revisions the good that flashes before me is in the context of preparing fish and game and any of the naïve or embarrassing stuff I'm able with wild abandon to simply cut from the pages and—just like that—from my life, too!

Yet, revising *Gray's Fish Cookbook* and turning it into *The New Gray's Fish Cookbook* was still not nearly so drama-ridden as it was for my wild game cookbook, even though *Fish*, too, is nearing having been written twenty-five years ago and only my second book. Where game is complicated, full of pomp and circumstance and is exotic; fish is easygoing, commonplace, and straightforward. Where there is a lot of pressure on the handful of us who are considered experts in cooking wild game, there are tons and tons of very good cooks who freely share their knowledge when it comes to cooking fish. And there are several really famous chefs who all recite the same mantra—and reinforce my own feelings about fish: Cook it fresh, cook it simply, cook with flexibility. (And, I would add, try to use wild fish.)

Master Chef Pierre Franey writes, "One of the most important things in learning to cook—and in knowing how to cook—is flexibility." And he confesses that he prefers fish cookery to all others. In his book, *The New York Times 60-Minute Gourmet*, he says at the beginning of his chapter on fish "Some of the simplest dishes can be foods for the gods ... Remember, in any of these (recipes), simply choose a fresh fish and take care not to overcook it." When I was learning about cooking and writing about game, famous, mainstream chefs weren't able to provide their stamp of approval for those wild ingredients—wild game being forbidden in US commercial restaurants. Now fish, that's a snap to cook, we all grew up eating fish and watching our moms at the stove frying up fish, right? Well, not exactly.

It's hard to muster fond childhood memories of fresh, flavorful seafood if you grew up in the Midwest in the 1950s, as I did. Then a Midwesterner's *sea*-food, obviously, had to come from oceans far, far away—I'm certain via mule-train over mountains and deserts—and what that "fresh" fish lacked in pallor, it made up for in aroma. Back then for me the only alternative was innocuously configured into frozen sticks. Of course today air freight—and the now well-known environmental resurrection of the then fish-dead Great Lakes—has changed all that. Now Chicago restaurants offer "surf" that competes admirably with their famous "turf."

But as a kid eating a seafood platter was fraught with very real trepidation. From the scary shellfish—all encased in unwieldy, inedible armor, sometimes with claws and feelers—to those glassy-eyed fish, just a bit bigger than your pet goldfish. Had any of that stuff been any place but on a plate, your mother would have warned against going near it and never would have suggested eating it.

Then I moved east to college and had kind of a seafood epiphany. In part because I was desperately seeking sophistication—like learning to drink martinis or smoke cigars—acquiring a taste for raw oysters or lobster tail was, I believed, simply a requirement of a cultured palate. But a revelation brought on, too, by living on the coast where readily available, superfresh seafood was standard.

Yet perhaps the most sudden leap of understanding about why Chef Franey would consider fish the food of gods came when I had the good sense to marry a fisherman and take up fishing myself. Those wonderful edibles that go from the wild to the table in a matter of hours—whether the evening's catch of striped bass or just-dug Ipswich clams, the foods harvested from the ocean, I discovered, are a magnificent taste sensation to be aggressively explored.

A sport fisherman has a tremendous advantage and is instantly on his way to gourmet chef-hood because he not only has the opportunity, but his very purpose is to procure a wild and fresh fish. All food seems better tasting if it's eaten the instant we take it from nature. My farmer father walks between the rows of his vegetable garden at lunchtime with a jar of Hellman's mayonnaise tucked under his arm. His garden inspection includes a pause at the cherry tomato vine where he plucks the just-ripe and sun-hot fruit off one by one, dipping each in cool mayonnaise until he's finished lunch. He maintains it's the best way, the only way, to eat them.

With having a lock on wild and fresh there's then a quite natural progression to a third attribute: Cook fish simply. Given fresh, wild fish (and the desire to get back to the fishing) the fisherman's preferred recipe mode is usually quite simple. Who needs to invent complex cooking techniques involving sauces and long hours in the kitchen (egad, away from the water!) when you've got fresh and wild?

So what about flexibility? Since the fisherman never knows exactly the size, or maybe the species or, for that matter, even if he's going to catch a fish, he must remain forever flexible. He must approximate cooking time, improvise with ingredients and the proportions, and use his imagination and senses, rather than a fixed set of rules, to determine when the fish is edible. It demands imaginative use of what's on hand; it requires that the cook be creative—and it makes a better cook.

The summer I learned to make pastry dough, my cooking instructor was appalled to return home one evening to find on her doorstep a sad, gray little pile of pastry pieces. Clearly left by some frustrated student who preferred no further explanation, only the vague innuendo of the misshapen blob left as a kind of threatening hex. It's hard to make pastry roll out properly in the heat of the summer, especially without the aid of a cool marble tablet; but as my instructor explained, if your apple tart fails because the pastry won't roll to size, make an apple tarte tatin. Or, in the fisherman's world, if it's too hot to cook and there's barely enough fish to go around, make a seviche hors d'oeuvre.

Actually, to me, one of the truly illuminating aspects in all the many different fish recipes I've now read or written is that the methodology always comes back to the basics: grill, poach, or fry—add some sort of fat and seasoning. But assuming those basics, then everyone improvises, however subtly. At first glance, the recipes here may seem all too much alike. I believe that slight, little nuances of change in a recipe do nothing but underscore the value of simple and basic while providing an opening for the reader's imagination, and too, provide a haven for the individual's own likes and dislikes... as well as create a new recipe.

So the cooking is simple and easy and the fishing is, too (well, except for that picky trout), and it's not just pretty easy to do, it's easygoing. Usually fishing for me happens where and when it's hot and the atmosphere languid; clothes are minimal and shoes lost to the back of the closet. To go fishing, it's simply a walk to the lake or a troll in the boat—it's cruising. And there's a wonderful kind of potpourri quality to fishing. You have to be ready for surprises. You cast out your spinner bait and yes, it might catch the bass you were looking for or it might be bream on the end of the line. And for me, since I'm often ocean fishing, it could be a bluefish or a dogfish or a mackerel or that really ugly thing I caught once, a squawking sea robin. Your purpose is only surreptitiously to catch a specific species of fish; the aim is as much to be out there and to catch a good-eating fish, or lots of fish, or a big fish. For me it's all of the above. I confess to having a meat-fishing dominion to my soul; in another time and place I was probably a grizzly bear, or a horse, or a pig, or possibly all three. This is only with fish I catch—not store-bought—and I do catch and release trout (there always seems so few trout); and yes, of course, I'll put back a small-size striped bass, per the law. But the abundant ocean allows me the possibility to catch enough fish for dinner. And it's really not so much the fish itself that makes me a glutton—it's the fishing process, the wild places they come from, that makes them taste so fantastic. And as for cooking fish, it's a shrug of the shoulders, a grin, and an "oh, la di da." It's perfecto!

Although the edits and refreshes to this book were easier than the game cookbook, it still needed be done to make this cookbook accurate. I don't mean accurate so much in terms of numbers of tablespoons or cooking time, although that was good to revisit, too, or because the world has moved on in its culinary sophistication—now you can actually buy sun-dried tomatoes everywhere! No, the changes are because, as I've said before in several of my other books, good cookbooks have a personality and often are a straightforward reflection of a place or culture or of the author's character. This cookbook is a reflection of me, here and now, not just me when I was thirty-something and wrote the first edition, but me as a sixty year old—and now a long-time fisherman. If a cookbook is good, has that character, it has gone beyond the primary purpose of instruction and moved on to entertain and inspire. This is accomplished by revealing bias, passion, inspiration, humor, and probably even frailty, those human traits that combine to create an identity, and which are much more robust now that I'm sixty.

And yes and hurrah, this is done all in a milieu of cooking and eating wild.

Salmon

Salmon is a wonderful fish. Whether you fish for Atlantic or Pacific salmon or pull them out of Lake Michigan, their energy and excitement in the water are unmistakable. A beautiful, flavorful fish that lends itself to many varied recipes, salmon is surely as interesting and fun in the kitchen as in the water—except when it's to be poached.

On a trip many years ago to Labrador we were lucky enough to bring home twelve beautiful Atlantic salmon. Obviously recipe versatility was called for, poaching being one of the clear and desirable choices. I learned quickly that you should always release the salmon that are over the size of 24 inches if you intend to poach them. In all of North America (and probably Europe, too) there does not exist a poacher large enough for any salmon I've had the pleasure of meeting riverside. I know this for a fact since I called every kitchen store in the world looking for a poacher over the size of 24 inches. Several of the recipes I found in my cookbooks called for poaching large salmon in the dishwasher sans soap of course (?!) This being too bizarre I spoke with my professional fishing friends. First, I talked with our French-Canadian publisher friend—a great fisherman—and the person who had accompanied us to Labrador. He'd gotten his poacher by welding together two stainless sausage containers found in a remote meat-packing house in northern Quebec—not helpful. So I then spoke with my cooking friends who referred me to a restaurant supply house in East Boston, but who commented that I'd need to own a successful restaurant before purchasing anything there since the prices would require that kind of cash flow.

No, I never found a big poacher. I curled my salmon up in a turkey roaster and cooked it just fine. But if you, too, have found that poaching a salmon has lost some of its romantic appeal—indeed, proved rather insulting to this beautiful fish—by cramming it into a turkey roaster, I hope these menus for poached salmon will provide a remedy and bring back plenty of *ooh la la* to the meal.

Whole Poached Salmon If You Must
Green Mayonnaise
Salad of Zucchini and Yellow Squash and Tomato
Grand Marnier Rice Pudding

Serves four

    Yes, I realize there are definitely times when poaching a salmon is the only conceivable cooking method. The cooked salmon is then good hot or cold, of course, and looks good and makes you look good. If you plan to poach the fish and serve it cold you may want to consider decorating it the way the guys in the tall white hats do. Let the fish cool after poaching it and peel the skin off the body. Gently scrape the thin layer of grey bits off with a knife. Layer halved slices of cucumber in rows over the body so the cucumber resembles large fish scales. Cherry tomatoes are nice for an eye patch and of course good ol' hard-boiled eggs can be used for the bordering. Use your imagination and plan on this taking a while. But, in my opinion, decorating is completely unnecessary if the salmon is going to be served to fishermen; they like the way it looks—dead-glaze eye balls and all—just fine.
    The rice pudding looks most attractive when served in a glass bowl.

WHOLE POACHED SALMON IF YOU MUST

   ½ cup vinegar
   2 qts. water
   2 onions, chopped
   1 carrot, chopped
   3 shallots, chopped
      Salt and pepper
   1 bay leaf
   1 tsp. thyme
   6 parsley stems
   3 whole peppercorns
   1 bottle wine (about 3½ cups)
   1 10-lb. whole salmon, gutted and scaled

Combine all the ingredients except for the fish. You may use red wine for a nice change. Cook this court bouillon 30 minutes and let cool. Wrap the salmon well in cheese cloth which has been rinsed and, if you decide to remove the head, be sure to cover the end with tin foil. Cook the fish on a rack with the court bouillon reaching just to the rack. Simmer at 200° and start checking for doneness at about 25 minutes—or about 8 minutes per inch of thickness at the fattest part. The salmon is done when the thermometer reads 135°.

GREEN MAYONNAISE

   ¾ tsp. salt
   1 tsp. prepared mustard
      A few grinds of pepper
      A dash of cayenne pepper
   4 tbsp. vinegar and lemon juice, mixed
   4 egg yolks
  2½ cups good corn or peanut oil
      A big handful of de-stemmed spinach leaves
   3 tbsp. shallots, chopped very fine
   1 cup watercress leaves
   ¼ cup parsley leaves

2 tbsp. dried basil reconstituted with a few tablespoons of hot water
Any herbs blanched in a small amount of water for 30 seconds and puréed.

Beat salt, mustard, both peppers, vinegar and lemon juice together. Add egg yolks. Whisk until foamy. Slowly add oil. Add spinach leaves, shallots, watercress and parsley leaves, and reconstituted basil near end of adding the oil. Finish up and season to taste. If adding salt, dissolve in a little hot water first. Or, it may all be made quickly and easily in a food processor.

SALAD OF ZUCCHINI AND YELLOW SQUASH AND TOMATO

¼ tsp. each of salt and pepper
2 tbsp. good vinegar
⅓ cup olive oil
1 tsp. good prepared mustard
Fresh basil leaves—the little-leafed kind, if possible, called spicy globe
2 tiny zucchini, julienned
3 tiny yellow squash, julienned
Corn oil or cooking oil
1 head Boston lettuce or 2 Bibb, cleaned
1 tomato, skinned, seeded, drained and julienned

First mix salt and pepper and vinegar and then add the olive oil, mustard, and basil leaves and zip in the blender for a second or two. Sauté zucchini and yellow squash in corn oil until they just begin to cook. Be sure they keep some of their crispness. Let cool. Toss with lettuce, tomatoes and dressing, or you can keep the squashes separate and lay the alternate colors out in groups on top of the lettuce. Taste for salt and pepper.

GRAND MARNIER RICE PUDDING

- ½ cup rice, cooked in water
- ¾ cup, plus 4 tbsp. Grand Marnier
- ¾ cup yellow raisins
- ¾ cup light cream
- ¾ cup milk
- Peel of 1 orange, grated
- 1 envelope of gelatin
- 4 egg yolks
- A pinch of salt
- ⅓ cup sugar
- 1 cup heavy cream

Rinse the cooked rice in a strainer under warm water and put in 250° oven to dry a little. Fluff with a fork a few times. In a small pot with ¼ cup water and ¾ cup Grand Marnier add the raisins and bring to simmer. Cook until raisins are plump and liquid almost evaporated. Combine the light cream and milk in a small pot and add the grated orange. Bring to scald. Remove from heat and let sit for 40 minutes to infuse the flavor. Strain orange rind out.

Melt the envelope of gelatin in a custard cup with 2 tablespoons of water. Set in small pan on low heat to melt. Whisk the egg yolks, pinch of salt, and sugar together. Add the milk and cream mixture to it. While whisking cook on medium-high, add dissolved gelatin and stir constantly until thick. It will become thick quite suddenly. Strain immediately onto rice and stir. Add raisins. Stir. Add 3 tablespoons Grand Marnier. Taste and add more if you like. Whip the heavy cream and add to it any raisin juice and 1 tablespoon Grand Marnier. Whip only to be very soft with no peaks. Stir the custard/rice mixture with a large rubber spatula, resting over a bowl of ice and water. Be sure to let the custard bowl touch the ice water. Stir constantly but lightly as the gelatin sets. Stir until a path through the center of the mixture remains bare for a second. Then stir in ¼ of the whipped cream. Mix well, then fold in the rest of the whipped cream. Gently turn into an oiled mold and let sit in the refrigerator until set. You can do this the day before. Unmold just before serving. Serve alone or with sliced berries topped with a little sugar.

Salmon Scallops
Watercress Salad
Potato Gratin
Grand Marnier Soufflé

Serves four

Using very good prepared mustards that are not too hot and that tout herbs on their labels is critical to making a good salad dressing. Some cities (Boston and London for certain) have stores where their sole purpose in life is to sell different mustards. Next time your rich brother-in-law goes to London, tell him he can make points by bringing you back some fancy mustard.

SALMON SCALLOPS

- 2 tbsp. shallots, chopped very, very fine
- ¼ cup cider vinegar or lemon juice, strained
- ½ cup very dry white wine
- Salt and pepper
- 8 ¼-inch salmon scallops, cut from fillets, about 2 lbs. in all
- 2 sticks or 8 oz. unsalted butter at room temperature

Combine shallots, vinegar, wine, a little salt and a grind of pepper. Simmer slowly until reduced by ⅓. This you can do ahead. Sauté the salmon very quickly in a couple of tablespoons or so of butter, to a slow count of 5 or 6 seconds each side. Remove to platter or plates. Spoon fat out of pan. Add the vinegar mixture to the fish pan. Scrape around for goodies and on very low heat whisk in the remaining butter slowly to make a foaming sauce. Taste for seasoning. Add salt and pepper if necessary. Serve hot over fish.

WATERCRESS SALAD

- 1 garlic clove, peeled and crushed
- 2 tbsp. wine vinegar
- 1 tsp. prepared mustard
- 1 tsp. soy sauce
- Salt and pepper
- ⅓ cup good quality olive oil
- Bunch watercress without stems, washed
- 2 Bibb or 1 head Boston lettuce, washed
- ½ head red lettuce, washed

Rub salad bowl with garlic. Combine in the blender the vinegar, mustard, soy sauce and salt and pepper and zip on high for a second or two. Add olive oil and blend again. Toss with the greens and serve with a crusty bread and butter and a couple of cheeses.

POTATO GRATIN

- 1 clove garlic
- 1 tbsp. unsalted butter, soft
- 4-6 Idaho potatoes
- 2+ cups cream
- Salt and pepper
- Nutmeg, whole to grate
- ¼ cup fontina cheese, grated (optional)

Rub a medium size baking dish with the peeled garlic clove. Let dry.
Then grease with the butter. Peel and slice potatoes very thin. Make a layer of potatoes covering the bottom. Cover with cream. Season with salt and pepper and nutmeg. Add another layer of potatoes, putting in the cheese here if you like, then more cream and salt and pepper, nutmeg, etc. Top with a layer of cream. Bake in a preheated 300° oven for at least an hour or until butter starts to bubble around the edge. Let sit 10 minutes at least before serving.

GRAND MARNIER SOUFFLÉ

- 2 tbsp. soft butter, plus some to butter the soufflé dish
- 5 tbsp. sugar, plus some for dusting
- 1 cup milk
- 3 tbsp. flour
- 1 vanilla bean
- Grated rind of one small orange (optional)
- 4 eggs, separated
- 4 tbsp. Grand Marnier
- 1 extra egg white
- Pinch salt
- Confectioners' sugar

Butter and sugar a 6-cup soufflé dish. Stir the flour with a tablespoon or so of the cold milk. Bring to a boil the rest of the milk with 4 heaping tablespoons of sugar and the vanilla bean. Remove from heat and let sit for 10 minutes. Remove vanilla bean. Stir in flour mixture (and orange rind if used). Stir over medium high heat until mixture thickens. Stirring continually until it just boils, remove from heat. Continue to stir. Add the egg yolks one by one to sauce. Whisking well after each addition, whisk in the butter and the Grand Marnier. Beat the 5 egg whites and a pinch of salt together until it reaches the soft peak stage. Add 1 tablespoon sugar and beat until stiff and a whole egg in its shell will sit on top of the whites sinking in only ⅓ of the way. Stir ⅓ of the whites into the milk, yolk, sugar mixture and then fold in the rest of the whites. Pour gently into soufflé dish. It should only be ¾ full. Cook in a preheated oven at 375° for about 25 minutes. Then open the oven door and quickly sprinkle the top with confectioners' sugar. Do this a few times for a glaze over 10 minutes. Soufflé will be done in about 35 to 40 minutes in all. Be sure it is cooked through. Serve immediately, of course.

Salmon Medallions with Black Olive and Basil Butter
Fiddleheads with Fried Bread Crumbs
Julienned Carrots
Poached Pears and Figs
Sugar Cookies

Serves four

In *The New Gray's Wild Game Cookbook*, there is quite a long description of the Chet Reneson method of cleaning fiddleheads. The method involves dressing in full sou'wester outfit and tearing down a long lake in a motorboat, holding up each fiddlehead as you speed along, in hopes of getting the chaff off. This description produced several letters from readers when I wrote about it in the original *Gray's Wild Game Cookbook*, either querying what the heck were fiddleheads or suggesting their own rather bizarre and unprintable techniques for removing the chaff from fiddleheads.

Fiddleheads are baby ferns, very delicious greens. It is possible to get the chaff off by plunging them in boiling water for a few minutes and then draining and rinsing and patting them dry on a towel that you intend to throwaway after the fiddleheads are clean. This must be repeated multiple times and is very tedious work. Try to pick the ones that are clean or find them already clean and in cellophane at your grocer.

SALMON MEDALLIONS

- 4 salmon steaks about ¾-inch thick
- 3 tbsp. unsalted butter
- Salt and pepper

To prepare the salmon medallions, first slice from a whole, cleaned salmon four ¾-inch steaks. This can be done with a still-frozen, but gutted, fish by using a saw. This has the advantage of giving you just what you need at the time and returning the rest of the salmon to the freezer for future use. Or, with a fresh fish, use a sharp knife and a cleaver to get through the backbone. Now with a pair of small pliers remove all needle bones from the four steaks. You can feel these by running your fingers over the flesh. Remember to do both sides. With a very sharp knife remove the skin and the center backbone from each salmon steak. Now you will have two pieces from each salmon steak. Lay the pieces down as if they were still attached and then flip one upside down so that the fat parts face each other and the thin parts go off in opposite directions. Now wrap the thin parts around in their natural curve (they will both be going in the same direction) and push four toothpicks in to hold together. You should now have a round, boneless salmon steak called a medallion. You can do all this in the morning and then put the medallions on a plate covered with some plastic wrap in the refrigerator until dinner. To cook the salmon, melt the butter in a fry pan over medium-high heat. Put the salmon in and cook the first side for 4 to 6 minutes, the second side for just a few minutes (remember fish continues to cook even though it's been removed from the heat, so remove the salmon when the center of each medallion is still a little bit darker pink). Place each medallion on a warm plate and season with salt and pepper. Put the compound butter immediately on top.

BLACK OLIVE AND BASIL BUTTER

 1 stick unsalted butter
 2 tbsp. dried basil reconstituted in 2 tbsp. hot water
 4 oil-cured black olives with pits removed and chopped finely
 Salt and pepper
 Lemon juice

Let the butter soften and then whip it till fluffy. Squeeze out the water from the reconstituted basil and add basil to the butter. Combine the butter and basil with the chopped olives. Add salt, pepper and lemon juice to your taste and then whip again. Turn the butter mixture out onto a large piece of plastic wrap and roll it up, shaping it as you roll into a log. Freeze for 24 hours, bringing it out of the refrigerator an hour or so before the salmon is cooked. Use a cookie cutter to cut the butter pats for atop the salmon. (The remainder of the butter can be used in soup or as a nice sandwich spread. Keeps one month in the freezer).

FIDDLEHEADS WITH FRIED BREAD CRUMBS

- 1 cup clarified butter
- ¼ tsp. chopped garlic
- 3 tbsp. hard bread crumbs
- Salt and pepper
- 1 lb. fiddleheads, cleaned of chaff and blanched
- 2 tbsp. unsalted butter

For the bread crumbs, heat the clarified butter and add to it the garlic and bread crumbs. Sauté until the bread crumbs are a nice golden brown and then season with salt and pepper. Now sauté the blanched fiddleheads in 2 tablespoons of butter until they are hot. Toss the bread crumbs and fiddleheads together and check for seasoning. Serve immediately.

JULIENNED CARROTS

- 8-10 nice sized carrots
- 2 tbsp. unsalted butter
- 1 tbsp. fresh parsley, chopped fine
- Salt and pepper

Scrape the outside of each carrot with a vegetable peeler and cut into 2-inch lengths. Now julienne the carrots into ⅛-inch sticks and blanch in boiling water for about 5 minutes or until just tender and then drain. Sauté the carrots quickly in butter, adding the parsley, salt, and pepper to your taste.

POACHED PEARS AND FIGS

- 1 vanilla bean, split
- 2 cloves
- 2 cups water
- ½ cup sugar
- ¼ lb. dried figs
- ½ lb. dried pears (fresh, still-hard pears can be used, too. In this case peel, core, and slice the pears.)

Bring to a boil the first four ingredients and let simmer 5 to 10 minutes. Add the figs, cover, and cook very gently until they are soft, about 45 minutes. Add the pears and continue to cook for another 15 minutes. Remove the fruit and reduce the syrup over a high heat by ¼. Serve with the syrup and crème fraîche.

SUGAR COOKIES

- 1 cup unsalted butter, softened
- ½ cup sugar
- ¼ tsp. salt
- 1 tsp. grated orange rind
- Dash of vanilla
- 2 cups all-purpose flour
- Sprinkles of cinnamon sugar

Cream the butter into the sugar and salt. Whip till fluffy. Add orange rind and vanilla and mix. Blend in the flour. Once well-combined turn the dough into a plastic quart-size bag and roll the dough in the bag so it is an even thickness and completely fills the bag. Place the dough on a cookie sheet in the freezer until firm, about 20 minutes. Remove from the freezer and let soften slightly. Slit the sides of the bag, peel back the plastic and cut with a cookie cutter. Sprinkle with cinnamon sugar, place on a cookie sheet lined with parchment paper and bake at 350° till just starting to brown around the edges (about 15 to 20 minutes or so). Repeat with the remaining dough (you may need to put it in the fridge for a couple minutes after rolling to make the dough firm again). Remove from the oven and let sit for 5 minutes, then with a spatula place each cookie on a cooling rack.

Fresh Mozzarella Slices
Grilled Whole Salmon
Rice Pilaf
Peas and Artichoke Hearts
Raspberry Tart

Serves four

A good homemade tart pastry is, to my way of thinking, one of the most difficult items to make. Little French girls learn at their mothers' sides and have the advantage of years of practice. Big American girls learn at the side of their cooking instructor and anonymously leave piles of grey dough on the instructor's doorstep in frustration and anger. If you master the technique for good tart pastry you will most certainly be rewarded by the oohs and ahhs of your guests. I have included a recipe for pastry dough in the Basics chapter at the end of the book (p. 219). But I do believe that pastry making is something that cannot be described in a cookbook; you must see someone do it. Consequently, if you haven't had the chance to observe an expert at work, use frozen Pepperidge Farm puff pastry sheets. They are a whole lot better than grey piles of over-worked dough.

FRESH MOZZARELLA SLICES

As a first course, thinly slice fresh mozzarella cheese. Drizzle good olive oil on it and sprinkle with cracked black pepper. Serve with homemade bread.

GRILLED WHOLE SALMON

Clean the salmon and remove the head. Also scrape the scales off. Wash the cavity well with fresh water and sprinkle the cavity with salt and pepper and your choice of herbs. Brush the salmon's skin with olive oil or butter. Heat the grill till very hot, a gas grill for 10 minutes. While this is happening, measure the thickest part of the fish in inches. Multiply that number by eight and that's your approximate total cooking time for both sides of the fish.

RICE PILAF

- ½ cup unsalted butter
- 2 cups rice
- 4 cups hot chicken stock (If using cubes to make stock, Knorr is preferable.)

Melt the butter in a large pan with a lid. Sauté the rice in the butter until quite hot and add the stock. Lower the heat to a simmer and cover the pan with the lid. Cook about 25 minutes depending on the depth of the pan. The rice is done when the grains are plump and separate and all the liquid has been absorbed.

PEAS AND ARTICHOKE HEARTS

- 2 7.5 oz. cans of artichoke hearts in brine
- 2 lbs. fresh peas
- 2 oz. pancetta, chopped fine
- 3 tbsp. unsalted butter
- Salt and pepper

Now more and more, I find artichoke hearts packed in glass jars. But if you can only find canned artichoke, then several hours before, drain and rinse in lukewarm water. Let sit in a bowl of cool water, changing the water at least twice and the tinny taste should be gone. Drain and slice into quarters. While you're waiting for the artichokes to bathe, shell the peas. Blanch in boiling salted water for a minute or two, drain and plunge into ice water. Drain again and set aside. In a large saucepan, combine pancetta and butter and fry on medium heat for a few minutes. Add the artichoke hearts and heat thoroughly. Add the peas and cook till hot. Season with salt and fresh cracked pepper.

RASPBERRY TART

- ½ lb. cream cheese (not whipped cream cheese)
- 2 cups heavy cream
- 3 tbsp. confectioners' sugar
- 1½ tbsp. vanilla
- Cheese cloth
- 1 recipe your best pastry or Pepperidge Farm Puff Pastry
- ½ cup red currant jelly
- 1 tbsp. framboise
- 1-2 pints raspberries

Do this the night before. First whip the cream cheese. Then whip the heavy cream together with the sugar and vanilla until it is over-whipped and great clumps fall from the whisk. Now mix ¼ to ⅓ of the heavy cream into the cream cheese and mix well. Fold in the remaining heavy cream. Rinse the cheese cloth in cold water and line a colander with it. Pour in the cream mixture and place in the refrigerator on a plate overnight. If whipped and folded well, water should ooze out onto the plate.

Preheat the oven to 425° for at least 20 minutes. Roll out the pastry and line a buttered tart pan with it. Prick with a fork and line the pastry with tin foil and fill with rice, beans or pastry weights. Put in the oven for about 7 minutes. Remove the foil and weights and sprinkle with granulated sugar. Return the shell to the oven for another 5 to 7 minutes or until the pastry begins to caramelize. Remove from the oven and let cool for a minute or two, then remove from the pan onto a cooling rack. This can be done several hours before if you like, and if it isn't too humid out.

To serve, melt the red currant jelly in a small saucepan with framboise.

Fill the pastry shell with the cream mixture and cover the top with raspberries, right side up. Paint the berries with jelly and framboise mixture and serve.

Salmon Hash Patties
Sage Bread
Three Green Salad

Serves four

I do believe that the different species of salmon vary from each other also in taste—as does farmed differ from wild salmon in flavor and texture. Certainly the taste of Pacific salmon is different from the Atlantic and even varies to some extent between the five species of Pacific salmon. (I have even had consummate Pacific salmon eaters tell me they could identify in what waters a king salmon had been caught by the flavor of the fish.) The meat of the Atlantic salmon is quite a bit paler than other salmon and seems to have a lighter, more delicate flavor. I prefer any salmon if it's wild, but especially wild Atlantic salmon, which is extremely rare to find these days. The wild Atlantic salmon population is so low that all commercial fishing is prohibited and you're a very lucky fisherman to catch even one Atlantic salmon a season by rod. So the Atlantics we generally eat now are aqua farmed. But for this recipe the best salmon to use would be the more hearty-flavored coho found wild from Alaska to Lake Michigan; or actually even better might be the salmon that already has been cooked and in your refrigerator and needs to be used up.

SALMON HASH PATTIES

- 1 very small onion, chopped fine
- 1 small celery stick, chopped fine
- ¼ cup butter
- 2 cups (leftover) cooked salmon, no bones or skin, and flaked
- 2 eggs, beaten lightly
- 1 large Idaho potato, cooked and mashed
- Salt and pepper
- Parsley, chopped (optional)
- Flour for dredging

Sauté the onion and celery in 2 tablespoons of the butter until they are wilted. Place the salmon in a mixing bowl with the cooked onion and celery plus the eggs and potato. Season with salt and pepper and a little chopped parsley if you like. Form into patties and dip lightly in flour. Sauté in the remaining butter until golden.

SAGE BREAD

- 2 cups lukewarm to warm water
- 1 tbsp. dry yeast
- 1 tbsp. sugar
- 1 tbsp. salt
- 2 tbsp. dried sage leaf, plus enough to sprinkle atop each loaf
- 5 cups or so of all-purpose flour (I recommend King Arthur Flour)
- Butter and oil for greasing pans

In the bowl of a standing mix master, fitted with a bread hook, add the warm water and sprinkle in the yeast, sugar, salt, and 2 tbsp. sage. Let sit for a few minutes until the yeast looks dissolved and foamy. Now pour in 5 cups of flour and mix at the lowest setting, usually marked "stir," until the flour is blended and then increase the speed to the next level, #2. Continue blending at this speed until the dough is well mixed, pulling away from the sides of the bowl, and forming a ball. Turn onto a floured surface and knead the dough for about 8 minutes. It should be slightly tacky to the touch but smooth and very malleable. Place in a bowl that has been oiled, turn the dough over in the oil so the top is oiled, too, and cover the bowl with a cloth. Let rise until it is double in size, about 2 to 3 hours. Punch it down and let it rest while you prepare the pan(s) for it to rise in again.

This recipe makes enough for a baguette and a loaf. I always make a baguette for the week's spaghetti night so I pull a handful of dough off and roll it into a big snake and lay it in one side of a baguette pan that has been buttered. The remaining dough I either place into a buttered loaf pan, pushing it into the rectangle shape, or form a ball with the dough, flouring it heavily, and put into a banneton, also heavily floured. Both the baguette and the loaf/round I cover with a cloth and let rise again for another hour or so.

The breads in the metal baking pans can first be sprinkled with sage and then go directly into a preheated oven at 420° for 35 to 40 minutes until golden brown. The banneton is trickier. I use a piece of parchment paper, floured, atop the back of a cookie sheet and careful invert the banneton and let the dough fall out. Often it loses its rise and I let it sit covered for another hour to rise again. Once the round is ready to bake I sprinkle it with sage and slide it onto a pizza stone that is in a preheated oven at 420° and bake it for 40 minutes or until golden. Once baked, I turn the baguette and loaf out of their pans—or slide the round on the parchment onto the cookie sheet—and onto a rack to cool. Let cool for 30 minutes or so before cutting.

If I don't plan to use the baguette that day I wrap it in foil and put it in the freezer to use another day. (It just needs to be taken from the freezer and put in a preheated oven at 350° for 30 minutes or so.)

THREE GREEN SALAD

- 3 tbsp. wine vinegar
- Salt and pepper
- 2 tsp. good prepared mustard
- ¼ tsp. garlic, chopped fine or squeezed through a press
- A dash of soy sauce
- ½ cup olive oil
- 1 tbsp. mayonnaise
- At least three different greens; endive, watercress, Boston lettuce or whatever is available to you
- 6 strips of cooked bacon

Combine the vinegar, salt and pepper, mustard, garlic and soy sauce. Add the oil and mix well. Now add the mayonnaise and mix well again. Toss dressing with the greens. Crumble the bacon into the salad and toss again.

Salmon Salad
Summer Popovers
Another Grand Marnier Soufflé

Serves four

Why do I have two Grand Marnier soufflé recipes in this book? Recipes have different styles and suit individuals differently. That's why so many cookbooks are sold. The end result for each of these soufflés is the same, a delicious dessert, but you may find one recipe easier and thus produces a more reliably and tasty result for you. Try them both and stick with whatever works for you.

I adapted this recipe for popovers from the magazine, *Cooking Light*, which true to editorial form found a way to reduce the amount of fat and calories in classic popovers and still make them delicious. I'm generally not too manic about cutting down on butter and fat, but this works and feels better in general as a bread that is perfect for a light, easy to prepare, summer meal.

SALMON SALAD

- 2 cucumbers
- 2 ripe tomatoes
- 2 small zucchini
- 2 tbsp. corn oil
- 1 cup cooked salmon, broken into chunks
- 2 tbsp. homemade mayonnaise
- 1 tsp. lemon zest
  Fresh basil, preferably small leaf
  Salt and pepper
  Lettuce

Peel and seed the cucumbers. Slice into ⅛-inch pieces; salt and let drain. Peel, seed, drain and coarsely chop the tomatoes. Cut the zucchini in half the long way and then slice into ⅛-inch pieces. Sauté the zucchini quickly in a little corn oil and let cool.

Combine salmon, mayonnaise, lemon zest, cucumber, and zucchini. Toss lightly, but well and season to taste. At the last minute, add basil and tomatoes. Toss carefully again. Taste for seasoning and serve on lettuce.

SUMMER POPOVERS

1 cup all-purpose flour
½ tsp. salt
2 large eggs
1 cup low-fat milk
1 tbsp. butter, melted
  Olive oil cooking spray
1 tbsp. olive oil

    Whisk together the flour and salt and set aside. Beat the eggs together in a medium-size bowl, add in the milk and blend well. Let the milk-egg mixture sit for at least 30 minutes until the mixture is at room temperature. This will make the popovers puff better if the milk and eggs aren't too cold. Now gradually add in the flour mixture, whisking until well combined and then stir in the melted butter.
    If you own popover cups use those, otherwise muffin tins work just fine; just remember to shorten the cooking time by about 5 minutes as the muffin tins produce smaller popovers. Spray the cups with the olive oil, and then add a drop of good green olive oil to the bottom of each cup. Place the unfilled cups in a preheated 375° oven for 5 minutes. Remove the hot cups and divide the batter evenly between each of the cups (if you are using popover cups you'll fill about nine of them). Bake for 40 minutes—remember less if using a muffin tin—or until nicely golden and puffy. Don't check on the popovers by opening the oven door—use the light to see if they look done. Serve immediately.

ANOTHER GRAND MARNIER SOUFFLÉ

    Butter to grease the soufflé dish
4 tbsp. sugar and some for dusting
3 tbsp. flour
1 tsp. grated orange rind
8 tbsp. milk
4 egg yolks
1 tbsp. vanilla extract
4½ tbsp. Grand Marnier liqueur
5 egg whites and a pinch of salt

Have ready a buttered and sugared 6-cup soufflé dish. In heavy saucepan mix 4 tbsp. sugar, flour, orange rind and milk slowly together. Bring slowly to a boil and stir till mixture thickens. Remove from heat and cool slightly. Then add yolks one by one, beating after each addition. Add vanilla extract and liqueur. In separate large bowl, beat salt and egg whites until they hold a whole uncooked egg, letting the egg sink in only ¼ to ⅓ of the way. Stir ⅓ of the egg white mixture into the base, mixing well. Then fold in the remaining whites. Fill the soufflé dish with the mixture, tap on counter once to release any large air pockets and cook in a 400° preheated oven for 30-35 minutes.

Smoked Salmon Salad
Fried Broccoli
Fresh French Whole Wheat Bread
Fruit and Cheeses

Serves four

Fresh homemade bread is the best, but in the summertime when the livin' is easy and it's too hot to bake, store-bought fresh bread is the way to go. In France you learn to truly appreciate how fresh bread (that means only a few hours old) enhances the meal. The bakeries there bake bread twice a day and you buy your bread twice a day. I've read that an average French person will eat a pound of bread a day. I find this completely understandable having lived with their bread for a while. Although it is not in our tradition to go out twice a day for bread, it is possible now to find very fresh bread at local at grocery stores, usually first thing in the morning. This is worth the trip for this meal.

SMOKED SALMON SALAD

- 1 orange
- 1 red onion, peeled and sliced thin
- Olive oil
- 2-3 tbsp. Armagnac
- Salt and fresh ground pepper
- 4 portions of smoked salmon (about 2 cups)

Cut both ends off the orange and with a large, very sharp knife, cut away both the peel and the pith from the top to bottom. When finished, you will have a completely peeled orange. Now separate and remove the sections (a small knife is best to cut between the sections.) Place orange pieces on a plate and set aside.

Place the peeled sliced onion in a small saucepan with a lid. Add a bit of olive oil. Steam over low heat till partially cooked but still a wee bit crunchy. Raise the lid and toss in the Armagnac. Replace the lid and remove from the heat to steep for a few minutes. Divide the onion between four plates using your judgment as to quantity. You may not need it all. Season with salt and pepper. Top with the smoked salmon. Dribble with good green olive oil and place orange segments around the edges.

FRIED BROCCOLI

- 1 head broccoli, separated into florets with 1 to 1½-inch stems
- ½ cup flour
- Salt and pepper
- Grated lemon zest from 1 lemon
- 1 beaten egg
- Milk to moisten to the right texture
- Olive oil for frying

Blanch the broccoli in boiling water until it is almost tender, but not quite. Refresh the broccoli in ice water, drain and let dry. Now combine the flour, salt and pepper, lemon zest, egg and enough milk so the mixture is a good-consistency batter. Dip the broccoli in the batter. Fry in hot olive oil. Drain on paper towels and serve at once with a lemon wedge if desired.

Salmon Calzone
Green Salad
Brownies

Serves four

Brownies were my first foray into cooking—and they came from a box mix. Brownies remain one of my favorite desserts—yes, from a box—perhaps because they were my first. But should you have the time and inclination, these from scratch are fabulous, too.

Calzone is a loaf of bread with stuff in the middle (usually meat or fish). It is very good for Sunday suppers or mother-in-law lunches or cold in a picnic driving to your favorite fishing spot.

SALMON CALZONE

- 1⅓ cups lukewarm to warm water
- ½ tbsp. dry yeast
- ½ tbsp. sugar
- ½ tbsp. salt
- 3 tsp. dried tarragon, revived
- 2⅔ cups all-purpose flour (I recommend King Arthur Flour)
- ⅓ cup whole wheat flour
- 1 small onion, chopped fine and sautéed in 2 tbsp. butter
- 1½ cups cooked salmon, broken into pieces
- ⅔ cup cooked rice
- ⅓ cup white wine, seasoned with salt and pepper
- 1 tbsp. chopped parsley
  Salt and pepper
  Butter and oil for greasing pans

In the bowl of a standing mix master, fitted with a bread hook, add the warm water and sprinkle in the yeast, sugar, salt, and 2 teaspoons of the tarragon. Let sit for a few minutes until the yeast looks dissolved and foamy. Now pour in the whole wheat flour and mix at the lowest setting, usually marked "stir," until the flour is blended and then add the white flour slowly until you can increase the speed to the next level, #2. Continue blending at this speed until the dough is well mixed, pulling away from the sides of the bowl, and forming a ball. Turn onto a floured surface—add more white flour if it is too sticky—and knead the dough for about 8 minutes. It should be slightly tacky to the touch but smooth and very malleable. Place in a bowl that has been oiled, turn the dough over in the oil so the top is oiled, too, and cover the bowl with a cloth. Let rise until it is double in size, about 2 hours. Punch down and roll out into a 3-by-12-inch rectangle. Let rest while you sauté the chopped onion and mix all together with the salmon, cooked rice, wine, parsley and the remaining revived teaspoon of tarragon. Taste for seasoning. Spread on bread and close bread up, tightly pinching seam. Flip so seam is on the bottom. Let rise about 1 hour and bake in a 425° preheated oven (on tiles or a stone if you have them) on the bottom oven shelf for about 35 to 40 minutes. Let cool to room temperature before serving.

THE BEST BROWNIES

- 2 oz. unsweetened chocolate
- 1 stick unsalted butter
- 1 cup sugar
- 2 eggs
- 1 tsp. vanilla
- ¼ cup flour
- ¼ tsp. salt
- 1 cup chopped walnuts

Preheat oven to 325°. Melt together the chocolate and butter and then stir in the sugar. Beat together the eggs and vanilla and add them to the chocolate mixture. Now quickly stir in the flour, salt and chopped nuts. Spread in greased 8-by-8-inch pan and bake 40 to 45 minutes at 325°. Do not overcook or they will be dry. Cake tester should just come out clean. Let cool in pan. Then cut in squares and remove. The first brownie will be hard to get out and may stick and crumble. Do not be deterred. These are the best brownies.

Saltwater Fish

One of the great advantages of being a fisherman is that when you bring back fish—unless something weird happened on the way home—it's always fresh. No matter how adamant the Dallas waiter is that his ten-pound lobster flown in from Nova Scotia is the best in the world, I know that the one-pound lobster I get from my friend Striker—who used to scuba dive for them off the beach of our Massachusetts home—is the best. Of course, this is not just because it's so fresh, but because now, as a long, long-time resident of New England, I have local knowledge about the fish that swim in my backyard. I've learned that the giant lobsters are not necessarily the tastiest, just as Ted and Donna taught me that the snapper blues—those 1- to 2-pound bluefish—are great grilled whole while the bigger blues should be steaked—and definitely need to be fresh.

I don't profess to know more than you about a fish that swims in your home waters. And you'll note that I haven't included here every type of sport fish that can be caught and eaten. I won't include a fish I know absolutely nothing about just for the sake of inclusion. With a fish I'm only slightly familiar with I tried at least to use some imagination and not just the same-old, same-old standard technique for cooking it—after all, redfish doesn't always have to be blackened.

Usually there's no better guide for the chef than the local lore. Ed and I were fortunate to be able to travel to France with our children for a two-week stay with some friends in a chateau. The meals were cooked by madame (the caretaker's wife) but we did the food shopping. One afternoon we purchased from the local market the only fish large enough to feed us all, a merlu. It was a rather ugly looking bottom feeding type of fish which turned out to be similar to our hake. Certainly a respectable fish but not one I would have spent much time on. Madame made a lovely court bouillon and then a simple beurre-blanc to go over it, a recipe I would have reserved for salmon. It was wonderful; she certainly knew how to cook her own local fish.

Now having said this, I do have one word of caution that must be thrown into this local lore business. I spent two summers—nearly six months—during my late teens working at a hospital in northern Newfoundland. I lived in the orphanage, which was next door to the hospital, and down the street from the fish docks and local fish cannery. I ate cod three meals a day, every day for six months. It certainly was fresh, certainly cooked by locals, and it certainly was terrible. I knew that the cod seemed bad in part because we ate it so much, but it was also because the cook had no concept of when the fish had finished cooking. Her adage seemed to be, when in doubt cook for five hours, and she was always in doubt.

Certainly "doneness" in fish can rarely be reduced to precise minutes of cooking, as with a cake. There're too many variables to each fish for that. Size, the thickness of the fillet or steak, the amount of water left in the fish and how cold it is all change cooking time. It is definitely better to learn to rely on seeing, tasting, smelling, and touching a fish for doneness. Always, always a fish should be cut into and tasted before serving. The first bluefish I ever had was served by a hostess whose gas stove had run out of propane, which she either didn't realize or just decided what-the-heck and served anyway. I nearly never ate bluefish again. Good sushi is wonderful, but somehow half-cooked fish is really revolting, so taste the fish to make sure it's done—or almost done. It can always be cooked more, but over-cooking is impossible to undo. The cooking times in this book are always to be regarded as approximates, and you will notice that in some cases I have not written a time. This is because your senses—seeing and smelling and tasting the fish—are better guides to its doneness than something cast into the words of a book. Don't trust books on this stuff, trust yourself.

Inshore Saltwater Fish

One time I went fishing with our doctor friend David Lebwohl on his 25-foot cabin cruiser. It had been one of those last-minute, it's-such-a-beautiful-day, let's-go-fishing, trips. Ed was on deadline and couldn't go, but I had only to bring along one baby—four-month-old Will—and find the right fishing equipment in the garage and then I was good to go. I was pretty used to fishing but rarely went fishing without Ed—especially saltwater fishing. And Ed was king of equipment in our household. He wasn't what you would call manic about the care of the hunting and fishing equipment. In fact he was what you really would call casual. Rust and saltwater corrosion were on intimate terms with several pieces of our equipment. But he did have the distinct advantage of knowing where in that great expansive morass of stuff in the garage even the tiniest fly would be hiding. No such advantage existed for me, however, so if the stuff right in front of me looked like it could catch a fish, I'd go for it. What did it matter if we were going mackerel fishing and I had grabbed a surfcasting rod, or if the lighter weight rod had white stuff all over the ferrules—they were both fishing rods, right?

The little rod had been really hard to put together, but I'd fixed it up with a multi-hook jigging rig, David had purchased some beers, cokes, and bait all at the same stop, and the baby was cooing in his little seat on the deck of the boat. Ready to go, we steamed out of the Gloucester marina. We spent an hour or two bobbing along, dipping the rods rhythmically, playing with the baby, watching him be lulled to sleep by the rocking of the boat. We talked, and ate, and drank coke and beer and let the sun beat on us. We would anchor and fish, then move and troll. David got a bluefish right off, then we waited a long time.

Suddenly, *wham!* David's jigging rig tugged and wiggled and bent and looked 25 pounds heavier; then, wham, mine did too! Scrambling for the rods before they'd flip out of the holders, we began to crank and pull and crank and pull. As the lines shortened we both realized we each had four fish on at once. We were both yelling gleefully back and forth about our prosperity, trying to drive the boat, and get the fish all inside the boat. Then I noticed that baby Will was crying. Strapped in his chair, he'd tipped over and lay on his stomach with arms and legs flailing, the chair on his back turtle-style. This was worse than a Chinese fire drill! With my right hand holding the rod and the left trying to right Will in his seat, David's fish flopped about on the deck. Then suddenly the end-piece of my three-piece rod fell off and was shooting down the monofilament. Okay, so I made a very un-motherly decision and left the baby floundering—so to speak— and went to save the rod tip. Leaning over the side of the boat to grab the tip-end of the rod, the boat lurched and there was a moment when I thought I'd be joining the fish in the water, instead it was the butt-end of the rod that was now in the brink. Now I was laughing so hard that I was totally useless when it came to retrieving the rod or landing the fish. David came to the rescue, boat-hooked the rod, jammed it back together, and brought the mackerel into the boat. I comforted baby Will.

Well-maintained equipment is probably a good idea both in fishing and in cooking. A rod that falls apart when it's catching a fish and a knife that is too dull to fillet a fish cleanly provide the same sad results, nothing good to eat. Both cooking and fishing have a tendency to produce equipment maniacs; and this, too, is to be avoided. There is as little reason to fill your kitchen with the superfluous pastry crimpers as it is to fill your tackle box with scent for plastic worms. Just give me my well-oiled green Penn reel and a barbeque grill and we'll call it dinner.

Grilled Bluefish
Grilled Polenta
Chicory and Escarole Salad
Cantaloupe Ice

Serves four

Polenta, a less-common starch than the big three, is a wonderful staple. A form of polenta, not using the cornmeal but a different grain, was carried by the Roman soldiers when they went to fight against Hannibal and his army. A food item that has stood the test of that kind of time has got to have merit.

GRILLED BLUEFISH

- 1½ sticks unsalted butter
- Salt and pepper
- 3 medium cloves garlic, chopped finely
- 2 tsp. finely chopped fresh sage
- 1-2 lbs. fillets, skin on

Make the compound butter in advance. Whip the butter until light and fluffy. Add salt and pepper, garlic and sage. Mix well and mound onto plastic wrap. Form into a cylinder and freeze for 24 hours. Bring to room temperature before using. On a preheat gas grill, place the fish, flesh side up, and cook for about 5 minutes. Then turn the direct heat off, leaving the other burner(s) on and let the fish continue to cook with the cover on about another 4 minutes, a total of 8 to 10 minutes. When done spread the butter over each fillet and serve.

GRILLED POLENTA

    A few slices pancetta, diced
1 onion
½ cup unsalted butter
3 cups milk
1 cup water
1 cup cornmeal
½ tsp. fresh grated nutmeg
    Salt and pepper

Sauté pancetta until just crispy. Save the fat. Chop onion very fine and sauté in the butter until translucent. Add the milk. Bring it to a boil. Combine water and cornmeal. Stir with a fork, then add to the boiling milk. Lower heat to medium and stir continuously until the mixture is so thick that a wooden spoon stands up in it. Remove from the heat and add the pancetta, nutmeg and salt and pepper to taste. Lightly grease a cookie sheet and spread the polenta into a ½-inch thick rectangle. Let stand until cool and hardened, several hours. Cut into squares and paint with melted butter and grill until hot and semi-toasted.

CHICORY AND ESCAROLE SALAD

1 tbsp. vinegar
    Salt and pepper
1 small shallot
1 very small garlic clove, chopped extra fine
⅓ cup light olive oil
1 tbsp. heavy cream
    Grated rind of 1 orange
1 head Boston lettuce, washed and dried
1 small head escarole, washed and dried
1 small head chicory, washed and dried
1 orange in sections and cleaned of membranes

Combine vinegar, salt and pepper, shallot and garlic. Let stand a bit to dissolve salt, then add oil, cream and orange rind. Mix well. Toss with lettuces and orange segments.

CANTALOUPE ICE

- 2 very ripe cantaloupes
- ¾ cup confectioners' sugar
- A pinch of salt
- Lemon juice to taste
- 1 tbsp. white rum
  (Make sure you have enough ice and salt for your ice cream machine)

Halve the cantaloupes and scoop out the seeds. Now scoop out the fruit and make sure you have about 1 quart. Purée the cantaloupe in a blender and then add the sugar, salt, and lemon juice sparingly until the mixture tastes right. Now add the rum and make any adjustments for taste. Place the cantaloupe mixture in the canister of your ice cream machine and place in the refrigerator for a couple of hours. Then freeze it in the machine according to the manufacturer's directions. For a nice effect you can pack the ice cream back into the cantaloupe shells.

Bluefish Broiled with Thyme and Noisette Butter
Asparagus
Perfect Tomatoes with Cognac Dressing
Raspberry Ice and Sugar Cookies

Serves four

Cooking bluefish fast and hot, as grilling or broiling does, is usually preferable over baking or poaching or any other method because bluefish is quite oily and needs the high heat to draw out the oil. For the same reason, bluefish is one of those fish that is best fresh—freezing it should be avoided if possible.

BLUEFISH BROILED WITH THYME AND NOISETTE BUTTER

- 1 stick unsalted butter
- 2 small size bluefish fillets
- 1 tbsp. thyme (preferably fresh)
- Salt and pepper
- Lemon wedges (Meyer lemons, if you can find them, are great for this)

Heat one stick of butter till foaming and then stir gently with your small size whisk over a high heat until the butter begins to turn a light brown. Remove it from the heat and continue whisking. If it begins to turn a darker brown turn into a cool pot and whisk. If it gets black, throw it out and start again. Paint the bluefish fillets with the butter and sprinkle with thyme. Broil the fish until done and then season with salt and pepper. Pour any remaining butter over the fish and serve with lemon wedges.

ASPARAGUS

- 3 lbs. asparagus (or 6 to 10 spears per person, depending on the fatness of the spears)
- Melted butter
- Salt and pepper

Cut or break off the bottom end of each asparagus stalk and peel with a vegetable peeler. Peeling asparagus makes them taste better, look less nasty and will impress your mother, so it's worth it.

Steam over boiling water until just tender when pierced with a fork. (Again, this will depend on the fatness of each spear and your own preference for al dente asparagus or not.) The asparagus should resist the fork just a little. Serve immediately with melted butter and salt and pepper.

PERFECT TOMATOES WITH COGNAC DRESSING

- 1 tbsp. red wine vinegar
- 1 tbsp. cognac
- 1 tsp. mustard
- Salt and pepper
- ½ cup light olive oil
- ¼ cup heavy cream
- 6 or 8 tomatoes

Mix the vinegar, cognac, mustard and dashes of salt and pepper. Whisk the cognac mixture together with the olive oil and the cream. Let sit for at least one hour. Immerse each tomato in boiling water for 10 seconds and put immediately into a cold water bath. Peel and slice the tomatoes and arrange attractively on a platter. Lightly sprinkle with salt and pepper and then dribble the dressing over the tomatoes.

RASPBERRY ICE WITH SUGAR COOKIES

- 2 quarts raspberries
- 1 cup sugar
- 1 tbsp. framboise (raspberry liqueur)
- Pinch of salt

Clean berries and purée in the blender. You should have one quart of purée. Boil the sugar in ½ cup water for five minutes, then let cool. Add the sugar syrup a little at a time to the purée, stirring all the time and occasionally checking the taste for sweetness. You may not need all of the sugar syrup; sweeten it to your taste. Add the salt and framboise and chill for at least 6 hours. Freeze according to your ice cream machine's directions.

For a good sugar cookie recipe, see page 35.

Broiled Striped Bass with Wild Mushrooms and Tomato
Peas and Artichoke Hearts
Chocolate Roll

Serves four

When I first wrote this cookbook in 1986 I wrote that "it sure is a good thing that grocery stores and gourmet shops are carrying a wider selection of mushrooms, both fresh and dried, because I was coming dangerously close to trying to learn to pick my own wild mushrooms. And I probably would end up dead."

Ah, how things change. For me, my first real brush with anything other than white button mushrooms came when I traveled to France in the early 1980s and visited the caves where exotic mushrooms grew in profusion. Unfortunately, back home availability was still often an issue. Except in special places such as the Seattle-type open-air markets, then I might find a few fresh exotics—portabella, wood ear, and enoki. Sympathizing with my mushrooming obsession a friend on a vacation in Italy risked the scrutiny of customs agents and smuggled home a gift of dried porcini. I was in love. I hydrated the dried porcini in order to add their essence into—everything! (I think I may have even splashed some behind my ears.) This was an interesting turn of events because porcini are wild, not a cultivated exotic. The exotics had been good to me but as a friend and purveyor of wild mushrooms said to me, "Portabellas are after all just big buttons." I was thoroughly hooked on the wild.

Of course, if availability was a problem for me with the exotics, think what it was going to be to get wild mushrooms. Plus wild mushrooms have an additional issue: not all wild mushrooms are created equally edible. Proper identification is critical and even when you learn mushroom idiosyncrasies from childhood there are still potential risks.

But fifteen years after the trip to France, the porcini, my ever-increasing passion for wild mushroom, there was quite clearly the need to learn about foraging for wild mushrooms. Fortuitously, not long after we moved to New Hampshire, I met Nadia. A Hungarian biochemist researcher at Dartmouth College who grew up in communist Romania, who knew quite a lot about classification and the European tradition of collecting wild mushrooms. She trained me to follow the golden rule of mushroom hunting: Know how to identify exactly just a select handful of wild mushrooms—preferably shown to you in the field by an experienced mentor—and know them well. Now each year Ed and I add to our foraging repertoire and rarely have to stoop to exotics or buttons—well, we'd never stoop to buttons. But wild mushrooms remain a very tricky business so despite the fact that they are spectacularly good, remember they are spectacularly good from a store, too.

BROILED STRIPED BASS WITH WILD MUSHROOMS AND TOMATO

- 1 lb. wild mushrooms—chanterelles, black trumpets, or dried morels, etc.
- 4 tbsp. unsalted butter
- Salt and pepper
- 1 tsp. fresh thyme leaves
- 1 tsp. chopped parsley
- 4 striped bass steaks, about ½-inch each
- Olive basting oil (See index or "Basics" chapter.)
- 4 large tomato slices, seeded and drained

Clean under a dripping faucet with a soft brush, don't immerse in water if possible, and cut in half the mushrooms larger than bite-size. Place mushrooms in a frypan over a high heat until all water has evaporated. Add in the butter and sauté until the mushrooms are just coated. Lower heat. Season with salt and pepper and add thyme. Cover pan and cook for 5 to 8 minutes stirring occasionally until golden brown. Season to taste and sprinkle with parsley and set aside.

Baste steaks lavishly with the olive basting oil and broil 6 to 8 minutes each side. (You can also grill the steaks, but cut down on the cooking time.) Place a tomato slice on top of each steak and brush with olive basting oil and broil again until the tomatoes begin to brown, 2 or 3 minutes more. Season with salt and pepper. Top with wild mushrooms and serve at once.

PEAS AND ARTICHOKE HEARTS

- 2 7.5 oz. cans of artichoke hearts in brine
- 2 lbs. fresh peas
- 2 oz. pancetta, chopped fine
- 3 tbsp. unsalted butter
- Salt and pepper

Now more and more, I find artichoke hearts packed in glass jars. But if you can only find canned artichoke, then several hours before, drain and rinse in lukewarm water. Let sit in a bowl of cool water, changing the water at least twice and the tinny taste should be gone. Drain and slice into quarters. While you're waiting for the artichokes to bathe, shell the peas. Blanch in boiling salted water for a minute or two, drain and plunge into ice water. Drain again and set aside. In a large saucepan, combine pancetta and butter and fry on medium heat for a few minutes. Add the artichoke hearts and heat thoroughly. Add the peas and cook till hot. Season with salt and fresh cracked pepper.

CHOCOLATE ROLL

- 6 oz. semi-sweet chocolate
- 3 tbsp. strong espresso
- 6 large eggs, separated
- ¾ cup sugar
- Dusting of dry cocoa
- Pinch of salt
- 1½ cups heavy cream
- 1 tbsp. confectioners' sugar
- 2 tbsp. liqueur of your choice

Melt chocolate with coffee in a double boiler and cool slightly. Beat yolks together and add sugar and continue beating until thick and light. Add chocolate to egg yolk, sugar mixture. Beat whites with a pinch of salt until stiff but not dry. Stir ⅓ of the whites into the yolk, chocolate mixture.

Gently fold the remaining whites into the chocolate mixture with a large spatula. Carefully spread mixture into a 10-inch by 15-inch jelly roll pan, greased, dusted with flour, and lined with parchment paper which is also greased and floured. Bake 10 minutes in a preheated 375° oven, lower the temperature to 350° and bake for another 5 to 7 minutes, until the top of the cake is firm to the touch. When done, set pan on rack and cover with a damp kitchen towel. Allow to cool 1 hour and spray with mister one or two times if necessary to keep the cake moist. Sift some cocoa onto a piece of parchment paper just a little larger than the jelly roll pan. Turn pan upside down onto cocoa-covered paper and carefully remove the bottom piece of paper used during cooking. Beat heavy cream with confectioners' sugar and liqueur until thick. Spread over cake and roll cake up like a jelly roll, leaving seam side down on serving platter. Chill several hours.

NOTE: Framboise would be a nice liqueur to use if you could add a few handfuls of raspberries to the whipped cream before spreading. Grand Marnier, Amaretto, etc., even rum is nice.

Bluefish with Lime Mayonnaise
Snow Peas with Peas
Boiled New Potatoes
Serves four

BLUEFISH WITH LIME MAYONNAISE

1 bluefish (about 5 lbs.) cleaned, gills and head removed, slashed
Several sprigs of thyme
Salt and pepper
2 large onions, minced
6 cloves garlic, minced
3 tbsp. unsalted butter

Preheat the oven to 375°. Stuff the cavity of the fish with a few thyme sprigs and season with salt and pepper and place in a large baking dish. Sauté onions and garlic in butter until onions are translucent but not brown. Pour over fish and bake 50 minutes. Flesh will flake when done. Drain off juices and save. If more than 2 tablespoons, cook these juices until reduced to 2 tablespoons and then strain and reserve for the mayonnaise. Remove skin and serve at room temperature with the lime mayonnaise.

LIME MAYONNAISE

3 tbsp. water
1 tbsp. fresh lime juice
½ tsp. salt
3 grinds pepper from a mill
3 egg yolks
½ lb. unsalted butter, melted
Grated rind of 3 limes

Combine water, lime juice, salt and pepper. Cook over medium heat until reduced to about 1½ tablespoons. Reduce heat to low. Add yolks and whisk until mixture is thick and white. Take off the heat and add the warm butter bit by bit. From time to time dribble in the juices from the cooked fish to prevent the sauce from becoming too thick. Just before serving with the fish, add the grated lime rind.

SNOW PEAS WITH PEAS

1½ tbsp. unsalted butter
2 lbs. fresh unshelled peas, blanched, refreshed in ice water and drained, or 1 box frozen peas
1 lb. snow peas, stems and strings from each edge removed and cut in half at an angle, then blanched, refreshed in ice water and drained
Salt and pepper

Heat butter to sizzling and add peas and snow peas. Cook just to heat. Season with salt and pepper.

BOILED NEW POTATOES

Allow 3 small potatoes per person. Sprinkle with chopped parsley and season with salt and pepper.

Broiled Weakfish with Mint and Garlic
Couscous with Wild Mushrooms and Chives
Your Nice Green Salad
Orange Jelly

Serves four

It was not until I was a grown-up that I discovered that in Australia (and probably in several of those other countries that are British derivatives) they call Jell-O, "jelly." I can't quite recall what they call our jelly, perhaps just jam. Anyway, it makes it handy that I can use proper English terms for this dessert, because who would want to say they were serving Jell-O for dessert?

BROILED WEAKFISH WITH MINT AND GARLIC

- 1 tbsp. plus 1 tsp. dried mint.
- 1½ sticks unsalted butter at room temperature
- Salt and pepper
- 1 tsp. finely chopped garlic
- 2 lbs. weakfish fillets
- Lemon slices

Reconstitute the mint in warm water. Whip the butter until light and fluffy. Add salt and pepper, garlic and mint. Mix well and mound onto plastic wrap. Form into a cylinder and freeze for 24 hours. Bring to room temperature before using.

Broil the fish about 5 to 8 minutes. Just before done put several pats of the butter on the fish. Return to broiler to finish. Serve with round slices of lemon, the centers removed and filled with mint sprigs.

COUSCOUS WITH WILD MUSHROOMS AND CHIVES

- ½ lb. wild mushrooms, depending on what you can get. Morels, chanterelles, porcini, all are fine.
- 10 tbsp. unsalted butter
- Salt and pepper
- 1 cup chicken broth—Knorr cubes are fine

1 cup couscous
2 tsp. fresh chives, snipped

Try not to wash the mushrooms more than necessary. Wipe dry and cut into bite size pieces. If mushrooms are tiny, leave whole. Sauté the mushrooms in 4 tablespoons butter until hot and well coated. Season with salt and pepper, cover pan and lower heat. Cook in this manner for 5 to 6 minutes, then remove cover, raise heat and evaporate liquid. Stir occasionally until mushrooms become golden brown. Remove from heat and let stand.

In a saucepan, bring chicken stock to a boil with 4 tablespoons butter and salt and pepper. Stir in couscous, cover pan and remove from heat. Let stand about 7 minutes. Mix in mushrooms, 2 to 3 tablespoons butter and fluff the couscous and mushrooms. Add chives. Season to taste and serve.

Serve with a gentle green salad. No harsh greens, no garlic, no onions.

ORANGE JELLY

1½ packages Knox gelatin
½ cup cold water
3½ cups boiling water
¾ cup white sugar
1 small can frozen orange juice
3 tbsp. fresh lemon juice
1 cup heavy cream
1 tbsp. confectioners' sugar
2 tsp. vanilla

Dissolve gelatin in cold water. Add boiling water. Stir thoroughly until gelatin dissolves. Add sugar. Stir again. Add orange juice and lemon juice. Mix well and pour into glass container and chill well. This dessert is somewhat soft compared to Jell-O. Whip the heavy cream with the confectioners' sugar and vanilla. Whip so that it is loose and could still be poured. Serve with the "jelly."

Redfish
Potato Flan
Salad of Bibb Lettuce and Bittergreens
Chocolate Cake

Serves four

This redfish is another version of that popular Louisiana recipe. It can be made in a skillet but because of the high heat necessary and the quantities of butter, you will probably have half the country's fire departments in your kitchen before you finish. So do it on a gas grill; charcoal is not hot enough. Preheat gas grill hot, hot, hot. For the salad simply wash and spin dry the two lettuces and use the basic vinaigrette listed in the "Basics" chapter on page 217. This is no ordinary chocolate cake, so chocoholics take note.

REDFISH

Cooking spray
4 fish fillets, ½-inch thick, sliced in half horizontally if they are too thick
2 sticks melted unsalted butter
1 tbsp. paprika
¼ tsp. each thyme and oregano
½ tsp. cayenne pepper
½ tsp. each white and black pepper, fresh ground
1 tsp. garlic powder
2 tsp. salt

Spray the gas grill with cooking oil and preheat until it is VERY hot, like 500°. Just before grilling, drown the fillets in the melted butter. Cover the fillets with the last six ingredients and cook 2 minutes each side. When you turn the fish, cover the cooked side with more butter and even more when it is done. This ought to make everyone sit up straight.

POTATO FLAN

- 1 medium-sized flan, a baking dish with straight (1½-inch high) sides
- 1 crushed garlic clove
- 6 tbsp. unsalted butter, softened
- 2 lbs. potatoes, peeled and cut very thin (use russet potatoes)
- Salt and pepper, fresh ground, of course
- 3 tbsp. chopped parsley (Italian parsley if possible)
- Grated rind of 1 lemon
- 1½ cups onion, sliced thin and sautéed in olive oil until just golden
- ¼ cup chicken broth
- ½ cup heavy cream
- Juice of 1 lemon

Preheat oven to 375°. Rub the flan with the garlic clove. Let the flan dry and cover the bottom and sides with the butter. Make an even layer of potato slices on the bottom. Season with salt and pepper. Now add a parsley, lemon rind and onion layer, evenly distribute and season with salt and pepper. Keep going and end with potatoes. Mix broth, cream and lemon juice. Season with salt and pepper and pour over potatoes. Bake at 375° for 1¾ hours. Serve hot or lukewarm.

CHOCOLATE CAKE

- ½ lb. (2 sticks) unsalted butter
- ½ lb. unsweetened chocolate (the better the chocolate, the better the cake)
- 1 tbsp. lemon juice
- 2 tbsp. orange liqueur (Cointreau)
- 1 tbsp. vanilla
- 10 eggs, separated
- 1½ cups sugar
- Pinch of salt
- Sprinkle of confectioners' sugar

Butter and flour a 10-inch spring form pan. Cut a 10-inch round of parchment paper and butter and flour that, placing it on the bottom of the spring form pan.

Combine the butter and chocolate in a saucepan and melt both over a low flame. Stir in the lemon juice, liqueur and vanilla. Remove from the heat. Separate the eggs and beat together the egg yolks and sugar until they ribbon lightly and then combine with the chocolate mixture. Beat the egg whites until they just support a whole raw egg without sinking, but are not too stiff. Then stir in ⅓ of the whites into the chocolate mixture. Fold in the remaining whites.

Pour the cake batter into the pan and bake in a preheated oven of 250° for 2½ hours. Turn off the oven and leave the cake in there for 30 minutes. Remove from the oven and let cool completely. Slide a knife around the cake pan, invert on a plate, and release the spring form pan. Remove the paper carefully and sprinkle with confectioners' sugar.

Grilled Lemon-Thyme Mackerel
Tomato and Eggplant Tart
Nice Green Salad

Serves four

Your green salad or ours; see the index or "Basics" chapter for ours.

GRILLED LEMON-THYME MACKEREL

- 1 stick softened, unsalted butter
- Salt and pepper
- Grated rind of 1 lemon
- 2 tsp. fresh thyme, plus 4 sprigs
- Dash of Tabasco
- 4 little mackerel

Make the lemon-thyme butter ahead. Whip the butter until fluffy and then add the salt and pepper and lemon rind, thyme and dash of Tabasco. Place in plastic wrap and mold into a log shape. Freeze until an hour before it's to be used, then remove to the refrigerator.

Butterfly fresh mackerel and remove head and tail. Do not baste, but put some sprigs of herbs such as thyme on the coals just before cooking.

Cook flesh side first and serve with several pats of lemon-thyme butter on each fish.

TOMATO AND EGGPLANT TART

For olive basting oil:

- 1 cup good olive oil
- 8 peeled garlic cloves
- 1½ tsp. thyme
- 1 bay leaf

Heat on low all four basting oil ingredients for 20 to 30 minutes. Remove garlic and keep for whatever.

For tart:

- 1 recipe pastry (yours, Pepperidge Farm puff pastry, or mine (see p.219)
- 3 cups (approximately) baby eggplant, cut into ⅛-inch slices
- Salt
- ¾ cup ricotta cheese
- 2 tbsp. finely chopped scallions—a little green included
- Pepper
- 1½ lbs. (about 10) plum tomatoes, cut into ⅛-inch slices—let drain while preparing the tart
- ¼ cup olive oil basting oil (see above)
- 2 tbsp. fresh basil cut in slices or 1½ tsp. dried and revived
- 1½ tbsp. fresh oregano or ½ tsp. dried and revived

To revive herbs, place in a small quantity of hot water. Stir and let sit for a few minutes and then use.

This tart may be done in individual tart dishes or one large round one or just laid out on a cookie sheet which can look very impressive indeed. Roll out pastry and butter dish. If on a cookie sheet, butter first or line with a sheet of parchment paper. Lay pastry on the cookie sheet and turn edges over to form a little rim. Let rest in refrigerator covered for 1 hour.

Slice eggplant and toss with several teaspoons salt and let sit in a colander for 1 hour to drain. Rinse in cold water and dry.

Mix ricotta with scallions and salt and pepper to taste.

Remove pastry from refrigerator and prick with fork all over except edges. Spread with cheese mixture and layout tomato and eggplant in overlapping slices. Make circles if in a dish or rows on a cookie sheet. Brush with olive basting oil and sprinkle with herbs and salt and pepper.

Bake in a preheated 425° oven for 15 minutes on the bottom rack.

Lower heat to 375°. Move tart to top rack and cook 10 more minutes or until top is browned. As soon as possible, but with all dexterity, remove tart from cooking container to cooling rack.

Serve hot, warm, or room temperature.

Pasta with Spinach and Artichoke Hearts
Grilled Mackerel
Summer Popovers II
Raspberries with Crème Anglaise

Serves four

Crème Anglaise can be refrigerated after you've made it and saved for instant great desserts as a hard sauce over any fruit.

PASTA WITH SPINACH AND ARTICHOKE HEARTS

- 1 7.5 oz. can artichoke hearts in brine
- ½ lb. fresh spinach
- 1 cup cream
-    Salt and pepper
- 6 oz. imported pasta in shapes such as bows
-    Parmesan cheese, grated

More and more you can get artichoke hearts packed in water in a jar, but if canned is your only choice, drain and soak in lukewarm water for 20 minutes. Drain. Rinse and soak again. Drain and cut into quarters. Wash the spinach, remove the larger stems and steam until just wilted, about 10 seconds. Drain well, press water out with a slotted spoon. Chop spinach medium fine and set aside. Reduce cream over medium high heat to ½ cup. Season with salt and pepper. Add spinach and stir well. Add artichokes, stir and taste seasoning. Cook pasta al dente. Season with salt and pepper. Add sauce. Stir well. Serve with grated Parmesan cheese.

GRILLED MACKEREL

- ½ stick unsalted butter at room temperature
- 6 anchovy fillets, chopped coarsely
-    Pepper
-    A squeeze of lemon juice
- 2 tbsp. finely chopped parsley
- 4 pounds mackerel, split and boned
-    Olive oil for basting (see p. 216)

Whip the butter until light and fluffy. Add anchovies, pepper, lemon juice and parsley. Mix well and mound onto plastic wrap. Form into a cylinder and freeze for 24 hours. Bring to room temperature before using.

Brush the mackerel with olive basting oil and grill, flesh side first. Just before removing from the grill, put several pats of anchovy butter on each fish.

SUMMER POPOVERS II

- 1 cup all-purpose flour
- ½ tsp. salt
- 2 large eggs
- 1 cup low-fat milk
- 1 tbsp. butter, melted
- Olive oil cooking spray
- Several tbsp. melted pancetta or bacon fat

Whisk together the flour and salt and set aside. Beat the eggs together in a medium-size bowl, add in the milk and blend well. Let the milk-egg mixture sit for at least 30 minutes until the mixture is at room temperature. This will make the popovers puff better if the milk and eggs aren't too cold. Now gradually add in the flour mixture, whisking until well combined and then stir in the melted butter.

If you own popover cups use those, otherwise muffin tins work just fine; just remember to shorten the cooking time by about 5 minutes as the muffin tins produce smaller popovers. Spray the cups with the olive oil, and then add several drops of the bacon or pancetta fat to the bottom of each cup. Place the unfilled cups in a preheated, 375º oven for 5 minutes. Remove the hot cups and divide the batter evenly between each of the cups (if you are using popover cups you'll fill about nine of them). Bake for 40 minutes—remember less if using a muffin tin—or until nicely golden and puffy. Don't check on the popovers by opening the oven door—use the light to see if they look done. Serve immediately.

FRESH RASPBERRIES WITH CRÈME ANGLAISE

    4 egg yolks
       Pinch of salt
    ¼ cup sugar
    ½ cup milk
    ½ cup cream
    1 tbsp. liqueur (Grand Marnier is good) or vanilla
    2 pts. raspberries

Whisk together the yolks, salt and sugar. Combine the milk and cream and whisk that into the yolks. Cook over a medium-high heat stirring constantly until it thickens quite suddenly. Remove from the heat, strain and then whisk until cool. Add the liqueur or vanilla and spoon the crème anglaise over the raspberries. Can be served hot or cold.

Offshore Saltwater Fish

We fished in a tournament once and really thought it was terrific fun. It was a bluefish tournament for Grady White boats. We fished over an August weekend off the coast of Lynn, Massachusetts and were trying to catch the biggest bluefish or the smallest bluefish or the best combined weight over the two days. We caught a shark. Not a mako shark, just a little dogfish shark. This was quite exciting to our hosts who explained that in England, where they'd immigrated from, the fish in "fish and chips" was dogfish. We fried and ate it the first night of the tournament—a boneless and absolutely delicious fish.

We did actually catch some bluefish, too. Not enough to win the tournament but enough to learn a few things. In the last hour of the tournament I thought I was beginning to see an important correlation between the number and size of the fish being caught and the number of gin and tonics being drunk. It was something about catching more and bigger fish during cocktails? At the time, that correlation was very clear and revelatory, but I can't remember it now. What I do remember clearly is the care we took once we caught the fish and how quickly its freshness appeared to fade. Because we were trying to keep the weight of the fish up, we avoided letting the fish bleed (no bonks on the head) and it was immediately iced. Even at this, the weight dropped dramatically, about 25%, from the time it was caught and weighed to the time it had travelled five hours to the dock and was weighed. When photographing, you find the colors of the fish are the best and brightest while it is still alive—the colors fade with every passing minute after death. Certainly the taste must change as each hour passes, too, and it reminds me how lucky we fisherman are to have access to the very freshest.

Of course, the quality of flavor as it relates to the freshness of fish is not a particularly novel concept, just one that is uniquely within the fisherman's control and consequently should be managed properly. There is one other interesting observation I can make about these big saltwater fish. When it comes to almost all meat, size and age of the animal has more to do with the good flavor than does freshness. A large old buck whitetail is not nearly as tasty as the small tender antelope, or mutton versus spring lamb. This is not true with these large saltwater fish. A smaller tuna does not taste perceptibly better than one that weighs 75 pounds more. The consistency in the flavor of the big, fresh fish is one reason they are such a pleasure to cook.

Japanese Leftover Tuna
Sautéed Watercress
Melon and Fortune Cookies

Serves four

When I was working on the 75th anniversary edition of the *Joy of Cooking* I took the opportunity to try many of the recipes, not just the game and fish recipes I was hired to edit. So I experimented with making my own fortune cookies. In general I think homemade cookies are always better than store-bought, but I also thought this would be such a hoot to write my own little fortunes, tailored to my guests, and wrap them in the cookie dough. The night before I was to make the cookies Ed and I spent cocktail hour writing what we thought were hilarious fortunes. Well, it was funny to us, but our guests didn't really laugh very much. To make it worse, the cookies themselves weren't even that good. So it turned out to be a lot of work and not really worth it.

I recommend buying the fortune cookies for this menu and have your guests read their fortune aloud, adding the words "in bed" to the end of each and every fortune: "You will meet a tall, dark and handsome stranger—in bed." Or, "Soon you will find prosperity—in bed." You get the idea. And those fortunes really make 'em laugh.

JAPANESE LEFTOVER TUNA

Leftover cooked tuna—as much as you have. If little, add more of the rest of the ingredients; if a lot, decrease ingredients.
Pepper
Soy sauce
3 cans water chestnuts, drained and sliced
Sesame oil
1 bag imported Japanese noodle (called soba). Available in good grocery and health food stores (a buckwheat and wheat noodle).
Fresh lemon grass, dill or your choice of herbs
Ponzu sauce or similar sauce

Break up the tuna into small pieces. Season with pepper and soy. Sauté the water chestnuts in sesame oil and set aside. Cook noodles in water according to directions and then season with sesame oil, soy, and lemon grass, or other seasoning. Toss with fish. Serve with ponzu sauce.

SAUTÉED WATERCRESS

3 bunches of watercress, washed
3-4 tbsp. unsalted butter
Salt and pepper

Take each bunch of watercress and cut into 2-inch lengths (the bunches should be cut approximately into thirds). Sauté the watercress in the hot butter for a second or two, then add the lid for two minutes. Remove the lid, season with salt and pepper and a little more butter and serve.

Fresh Tuna Steaks
Pizza
Nice Green Salad
Blueberries with Crème Anglaise

Serves four

Fresh tuna is one of the great fish-eating experiences; go out of your way to obtain some. This goes for fresh mozzarella as well. It is really a different cheese from the mozzarella you get in the plastic bags in the supermarket (this is true also of Parmesan cheese) and fresh mozzarella will make your pizza exceptional. See p. 229 for a nice green salad.

FRESH TUNA STEAKS

2 lbs. fresh tuna steaks
Any of the compound butters you still have in the refrigerator, especially red pepper butter (p. 87) or lemon and garlic butter.

Grill the steaks about 6 minutes on the first side, 5 on the second. Just before the steaks are done, put some of the butter on each steak and then again when you are just about to serve it.

PIZZA

- ¾ cup lukewarm water
- ½ tsp. dry yeast
- ½ tsp. honey
- ½ tsp. salt
- 2 cups all-purpose flour
- ¼ cup olive oil
- ¾ cup mozzarella, grated—fresh if possible. If fresh, thin slices are fine.
- 2 tbsp. basil, roughly chopped
- 4-6 tomatoes, peeled, seeded and sliced
- Salt and pepper—fresh ground or hot red pepper flakes

In the bowl of a mix-master fitted with a dough hook, add the warm water, yeast, honey, and salt. Stir and let stand until the yeast looks a little foamy, about 5 minutes. Add in the flour and mix on the "stir" setting. Increase the speed while the flour is still being blended and drizzle in the olive oil and mix until dough is formed. Turn out onto a lightly floured board and knead well for about 5 minutes. The dough will be oily to the touch. Form dough into a ball and place in a plastic bag and let sit overnight, or at least 6 hours, in the refrigerator. Remove the dough from the fridge and divide in half, placing each half on its own piece of parchment paper measuring about 12 to 14 inches long and dusted with flour. Form each piece of dough into a disk and cover with plastic wrap. Let dough sit 15 minutes before rolling out into thin circles. Slide the parchment paper with each pizza round onto the back of a cookie sheet. Put your toppings on. If you use fresh mozzarella, put the cheese on first, then the basil, then the tomatoes, and then the pepper. Bake each pizza one at a time, by again carefully sliding the loaded pizza atop the paper onto a stone or bricks in a preheated 500° oven. Bake 8 to 10 minutes or until crust is golden. Slide cooked pizza back onto the cookie sheet and then onto a cutting board to slice. Repeat to cook the second pizza and serve. (If you want to serve just one pizza, roll out both dough disks but put toppings on just one of the rounds. After you've cooked the pizza with toppings and removed it from the oven, slide the second dough round onto the stone and let bake 2 minutes. Remove and freeze. Before using, let defrost 30 minutes before adding toppings. Bake as above.)

BLUEBERRIES WITH CRÈME ANGLAISE

- ⅛ tsp. salt
- 4 yolks
- ¼ cup sugar
- ½ cup milk
- ½ cup heavy cream
- 1 tbsp. liqueur or vanilla (Grand Marnier is good)
- 4 cups blueberries, washed and picked over

Whisk together the salt, yolks and sugar. Combine the milk and cream and whisk that into the yolks. Cook over a medium-high heat stirring constantly until it thickens quite suddenly. Remove from the heat, strain and then whisk until cool. Add the liqueur or vanilla and spoon the crème anglaise over the blueberries and serve.

Fried Pasta with Water Chestnuts
Grilled Tuna with Lemon Butter
Salad of Melon, Pears and Cucumbers

Serves four

I discovered to my horror that good oils can go rancid. This seems to be particularly true of the more delicate oils such as hazelnut or walnut oil. Keeping them in the refrigerator is one solution, or splitting the oil and the cost with a friend so there isn't as much to use up is another solution.

FRIED PASTA WITH WATER CHESTNUTS

- ½ lb. pasta, farfalle (bows) are nice
- ¼ cup sesame oil, plus some to toss with pasta
- Splash of vegetable oil
- 2 garlic cloves, finely chopped
- 2-3 tbsp. ginger, peeled and julienned into match sticks
- ¼ cup soy sauce
- ¼ cup rice wine vinegar
- Pepper
- 2 cans water chestnuts, drained and sliced
- 4 scallions, julienned and blanched for 30 seconds in boiling water, then plunged into ice water and drained

Cook the pasta until just al dente. Drain well. Toss with a little of the sesame oil so the bows won't stick together and set aside. Heat in a frying pan ¼ cup of sesame oil with a splash of vegetable oil till hot. Add the garlic and ginger and stir for a few minutes. Add the pasta and fry it till the edges start to crisp. Now add the soy sauce and the rice vinegar a little at a time over the fried pasta, tasting the pasta as you add. This recipe is flexible: One time you may want more soy, the next more vinegar. You may also want to add more sesame oil. Add pepper as well to taste. Toss in the water chestnuts and fry a little more. Now add the scallions, toss and serve.

GRILLED TUNA WITH LEMON BUTTER

1 stick of unsalted butter, softened
2 tsp. lemon juice
1 tsp. lemon rind, grated
½ tsp. dry mustard
 Salt and pepper
4 tuna steaks at least 1-inch thick, about 8-10 oz. each
 Oil to paint the fish
 Several sprigs of rosemary

Whip the butter till fluffy. Add juice, rind, mustard, and salt and pepper. Whip till mixed well, then mound onto plastic wrap and roll into a cylinder. Freeze a night ahead then bring into the refrigerator a few hours before serving. Brush the steaks with oil and lay a sprig of rosemary on top of each steak. (Or if you are using charcoal to grill lay the sprigs on the coals just as you put the steaks on.) Grill until done, about 7 minutes on the first side and 4 on the second. Remove to a platter and sprinkle with salt and pepper. Top with pats of the lemon butter.

SALAD OF MELON, PEARS, AND CUCUMBERS

2 tbsp. red wine vinegar
1 tsp. mustard
½ cup hazelnut or walnut oil
   Salt and pepper
½ cup hazelnuts, toasted and chopped coarsely
4 pears
   Lemon juice
1 small melon
2 medium sized cucumbers
   Lettuce

Combine the vinegar, mustard, oil, and salt and pepper in the blender. Turn on high for a couple of seconds and then set aside. Toast the hazelnuts in the oven set at 300°. Remove and cover with a towel for 5 or 10 minutes, then rub off the skins and chop coarsely. Peel, core, and slice the pears and toss with a little lemon juice. Add slices of melon, about an equal amount to the pears. Peel, seed, and slice the cucumbers. Toss the cucumbers, pears and melon together with the vinaigrette and let sit an hour or so. Just before serving toss in the toasted hazelnuts and serve on a bed of lettuce.

Grilled Swordfish with Roasted Red Pepper Butter
Green and Purple Cole Slaw
Grilled Idaho PotatoesSummer Trifle

Serves four

Yes, this chapter suggests only one way to cook swordfish. There is only one way to cook swordfish and that is to grill it. Suggesting any other technique would be implying that other techniques might be good. It is too expensive and too difficult to catch to fool with other techniques. Go with the best.

GRILLED SWORDFISH WITH ROASTED RED PEPPER BUTTER

- 1½ sticks or 6 oz. of unsalted, room temperature butter
- 2 small red peppers
- Salt and pepper
- Small spot of Worcestershire sauce
- 2 lbs. swordfish
- Good olive oil for basting

Prepare the butter in advance. On a hot grill, roast whole red peppers until blackened on all sides. Remove to a plate and when cool enough to handle, peel off all the skin. Slice open and clean out all membrane and seeds. Chop roughly and purée in food processor. Season with salt and pepper. With electric mixer, whip butter until light and fluffy. Add pepper purée in small batches to see how much the butter can hold. You want to add as much as you can, but it will depend on how big the peppers are. When you feel it is right, season with pepper, and just a little dash of Worcestershire. Check taste and add salt if needed. Mix well. Mound onto plastic wrap and mold into a cylinder. Freeze for 24 hours and then bring to refrigerator several hours before using.

Baste the swordfish with olive oil and grill on a preheated grill.

Slice the compound butter in ¼-inch slices and give several per portion. I say just slather it on!

GREEN AND PURPLE COLE SLAW

3 cups finely shredded green Savoy cabbage
3 cups finely shredded purple cabbage
1 large carrot, grated
½ tsp. salt
2 tsp. prepared mustard
¼ tsp. ground pepper
1 dash cayenne
3 egg yolks
2 cups corn oil or good olive oil
1 tsp. salt
¼ cup vinegar
2 tsp. sugar
¼ cup sour cream
2 tsp. lemon juice
2 tsp. caraway seeds
1 tbsp. dry mustard

Keep the cabbages separate. Divide the carrot between them.

Now make a mayonnaise by combining in a bowl: ½ teaspoon salt, the prepared mustard, pepper, and cayenne. Let the salt melt and add the egg yolks. Whisk until frothy and well combined. Add the oil slowly in a dribble, whisking all the while, until the mayonnaise begins to thicken. Then you may add the oil faster. When finished, taste for seasoning and adjust. Add a tablespoon of hot water to finish it off. This also can be made in a food processor. Now add the remaining 7 ingredients—making sure to dissolve the salt in the vinegar first to better dissolve it—to the mayonnaise and divide between the two cabbages. Mix well and taste for seasoning. You will want a nice sweet sour taste. Grate a little black pepper over each and chill for several hours. Mix again before serving a heaping spoonful of each color of dressed cabbage per plate.

GRILLED IDAHO POTATOES

8 peeled garlic cloves
1 cup good olive oil
1½ tsp. thyme
1 bay leaf

3 Idaho potatoes, sliced thinly lengthwise
Salt and pepper

Make a basting oil by combining the garlic, oil, thyme, and bay leaf and heating on low for 20 to 30 minutes. Remove garlic and bay leaf. Baste the potato slices with the basting oil and grill about 10 minutes total. Season with salt and pepper just before serving.

(The softened garlic can be used for whatever your taste buds tell you, i.e. smearing on the potatoes once grilled or on the swordfish before you add the red pepper butter or for the cook to halve atop a piece of French bread.)

SUMMER TRIFLE

2 cups light cream
5 egg yolks
½ cup sugar
Pinch of salt
Framboise or rum
1 sponge cake (store-bought is okay)
Raspberry jam (optional)
2 pints raspberries
Grated orange zest (optional)

Make a custard by mixing cream, yolks, sugar, and salt together in heavy saucepan. Over a medium-high heat, stir the mixture constantly until it thickens (which it will do quite suddenly, just as a cloud of steam rises from the surface). Remove from heat and pour through fine strainer into bowl and whisk to stop cooking. Cool, stirring occasionally and add framboise to taste.

In your best glass bowl put a layer of sponge cake with jam on it if you like. Spoon in cool custard just to cover. Spread profusely with raspberries (grate on a little orange zest if you like). Add more cake, then more custard, and finish with raspberries. Be sure the berries of each layer show off in an orderly manner through the glass. Chill overnight.

Grilled Swordfish with Garlic Butter
Panzanella Salad
Strawberry Sherbet

Serves four

When I call for good olive oil in a recipe, this is not done casually. There are terrific differences in olive oils. It is much like wine, and like wine, quality should be matched to the usage and occasion. For everyday salad use, I use everyday olive oil. But when the queen comes to lunch, it better be a good green virgin olive oil. And when you are going to baste a swordfish steak it better be good oil.

GRILLED SWORDFISH WITH GARLIC BUTTER

- 1½ sticks unsalted butter
- 2 tsp. chopped garlic
- 1 tsp. lemon rind, grated
- Salt and pepper
- 1 or 2 swordfish steaks (depending on size) about 1½-inch thick
- Good olive oil for basting

At least 24 hours before, prepare the compound butter. Whip the butter till fluffy, then add the garlic, lemon zest and salt and pepper to taste. Mound onto a piece of plastic wrap and shape into a cylinder. Place in the freezer the day before, then take out and bring to room temperature just before serving.

Paint the swordfish with a good olive oil, then grill. Serve with generous amounts of garlic butter on each serving.

PANZANELLA SALAD

- 8 thick slices day-old Italian or French bread
- ½ cup chicken stock
- 3 tbsp. butter
- 2 tomatoes, peeled, seeded, and coarsely chopped

1 medium cucumber, seeded and chopped
1 small red onion, chopped
1 head romaine lettuce
   A few bitter greens, such as chicory or escarole
   Shredded fresh basil leaves
   A good vinaigrette—your own, or see page 217
   Salt and pepper

Cut the bread into large cubes and dribble the stock over the cubes and toss. Fry in butter until crisp and let cool. Combine all remaining ingredients and toss with the vinaigrette. Check for salt and pepper and let sit a little to meld the flavors. Add croutons and toss and serve.

STRAWBERRY SHERBET

1 qt. ripe strawberries, hulled
   Squeeze of lemon juice
   Tiny pinch of salt
   Dash of framboise or white rum
1½ cups sugar
1½ cups water
¾ cup whole milk
2 tbsp. water
1 tsp. gelatin
   (Enough kosher salt and ice cubes for your ice cream machine)

Purée the fruit and add the lemon juice, salt and framboise. In a small saucepan combine the sugar and water and heat until the sugar is completely dissolved. In a bowl, pour the sugar water and the strawberry purée and add in the milk. In the saucepan put the 2 tablespoons of water and stir in the gelatin and let it sit until the gelatin has plumped up—about a minute or two. Then heat it gently so there is no graininess. Stir in the gelatin now to the fruit-milk mixture, cover the bowl with plastic wrap, and refrigerate for at least six hours until it is very cold. Then freeze it according to the instructions with your ice cream maker. Serve with cookies.

Corn Chowder
Grilled Swordfish Steaks
Artichokes
Apricot Ice

Serves four

If you have access to the little tiny artichokes, they would be good to use in this menu instead of the large artichokes listed in the recipe. I used to be able to find only the tiny chokes from California in Boston's Italian North End in the spring. Now they are available in good grocery stores, too, but still only at certain times of the year. Amazing how much has changed in the food world in 25 years!

CORN CHOWDER

6 tbsp. unsalted butter
1 large onion, chopped fine
1 small rib celery, chopped fine
2-3 potatoes, peeled and diced
1 large green pepper, diced
1 tbsp. bacon fat
2 qts. light cream
½ bay leaf
   Salt and pepper
   Pinch basil
2½ cups cooked corn

In 4 tablespoons of the butter, sauté the onion and celery until translucent. Add potatoes and green pepper. Toss in bacon fat, remaining butter and add light cream. Add bay leaf, some salt and pepper and a pinch of basil. Let simmer until potatoes are done, approximately 30 minutes. Add 2½ cups corn and taste for seasoning.

If you wish to have a thicker soup: just before serving, mix 4 tablespoons cornstarch with ⅔ cup of the soup. Stir and add mixture back into the hot soup. Stir gently. Bring to a boil and serve.

Garnish each soup plate first with:

> ¼ lb. cooked ham, diced and sautéed and divided among the plates
> Some finely chopped pimento

Sprinkle the top of the soup with chopped parsley.

GRILLED SWORDFISH STEAKS

> 4 good-sized swordfish steaks
> Olive oil
> Cracked pepper
> 4 tbsp. butter, melted
> Several Meyer lemon wedges

Baste swordfish steaks with olive oil and a few grinds of pepper. Grill on a preheated grill. Serve with Meyer lemon wedges and drizzle melted butter over the swordfish steaks.

GRILLED ARTICHOKES

> 4 large artichokes
> Olive oil
> Melted butter for dipping
> Salt
> Lemon slices for butter

Trim stem of artichokes to ½-inch. Slice off the tops with a knife and then with a pair of scissors cut off each sharp thorn, about ⅛ to ¼ of the leaf. Steam for 30 to 45 minutes. They are done when a leaf pulls off easily, and you want them to be done. When cool enough to handle, cut into quarters and remove the choke. Paint with olive oil and grill to desired brownness. Serve with melted butter, salted to taste, and lemon slices.

APRICOT ICE

    4 7.5-oz. cans of apricot halves in heavy syrup.
         Drain well and reserve the syrup.
      Pinch of salt
    2 medium size lemons for the juice
    1 tbsp. white rum
      Fresh mint leaves (optional

Purée the apricots in a food processor. Add a pinch of salt, squeeze the lemons and add ¾ of it, the rum, and about ⅔ cup of the apricot syrup. Taste for balance. You may want more sweetness (syrup) or tartness (lemon juice) or rum. Chill for a minimum of 3 hours. Then prepare as your ice cream machine says for ice. Decorate with fresh mint.

Kingfish with Lime Butter
Banana Chips
Tomatoes, Red and Green Peppers
Potato Cake
Real Tuttifrutti

Serves four

KINGFISH WITH LIME BUTTER

- 1½ sticks of unsalted butter
- 2 shallots, chopped very fine
- Grated rind of 2 limes
- 1 clove garlic, chopped very fine
- Salt and pepper
- 1½ lbs. kingfish fillets

The lime butter should be in readiness in your freezer for the happy moment when the fisherman comes home. So at least 24 hours before you expect the fish to arrive, whip the butter until fluffy and white. Add the shallots, lime zest, garlic, and salt and pepper and mix well. Check the taste and add more salt and pepper if necessary. Turn out onto a piece of plastic wrap, wrap it up and shape into a log. Freeze it, making sure it goes into the refrigerator one hour before serving.

Fillet the kingfish, leaving the skin on. Each fillet should be no more than an inch thick. Grill about 10 minutes skin-side down (do not flip) and check for doneness. After grilling top with pats of the lime butter.

BANANA CHIPS

- 3 or 4 medium-green bananas (about 1 lb.)
- 2½ inches of corn oil or peanut oil

Slice the bananas either lengthwise or across, whatever is your fancy, so the chips are ½-inch thick. Heat the oil till it is 375° and fry a few pieces of banana at a time, each batch for about four minutes. Make sure you turn them once during the cooking. They should be a nice golden brown when done. Remove to drain on paper towels. Serve with your favorite tropical drink.

TOMATOES, RED AND GREEN PEPPERS

   Olive oil
2 red peppers, seeded and julienned
2 green peppers, seeded and julienned
2 yellow peppers, seeded and julienned
2 tomatoes, very ripe, seeded and julienned
   Fresh coriander (cilantro) or chopped parsley
   Salt and pepper

Splash a bit of the olive oil in two frying pans and sauté the red peppers in one pan and the green and yellow peppers in the other. Sauté until they are just done and still a little crunchy. Add some of the tomatoes to each pan along with the coriander and heat through. Season with salt and pepper. You can stir them all together now or arrange in an attractive pattern on a serving platter.

POTATO CAKE

2 lbs. russet potatoes
5 tbsp. corn oil
1 freshly grated nutmeg
   Salt and pepper
2 tbsp. unsalted butter softened

Peel and slice the potatoes very thin, about $1/16$-inch thick. You can use a food processor or mandoline if you have one. Keep the slices in ice water until you're ready to use them, then rinse under cold water and dry on a kitchen towel. Heat half of the oil in a 10- to 12-inch skillet. Add the potatoes and sauté until lightly brown all over, about 10 minutes. Season with the grated nutmeg and salt and pepper. Stir again. Press the potatoes with a spatula or spoon into a flat layer in the pan and cook 5 more minutes, shaking the pan every now and then. Then invert the potato cake onto a lightly oiled plate and add the other half of the oil to the pan. Return the potato cake to the pan with the unbrowned side down. Finish cooking, about 5 to 10 minutes more, or until potatoes are completely brown but tender. Slide cake onto a platter and spread soft butter on top.

REAL TUTTIFRUTTI

- 2 grapefruits
- 2 oranges
- ½ pineapple
- 1 papaya
- 1 banana
- 8 tbsp. orange liqueur
- Fresh mint leaves (optional)

Cut the ends off the grapefruit and oranges and stand on end. Then with a sharp knife cut off the remaining peel. Separate into sections making sure the connecting tissue is left behind. Core and pare the pineapple half and cut into small pieces. Core, pare, and seed the papaya and cut into small pieces. Slice the banana. In a bowl combine all of the fruit and sprinkle the orange liqueur over it. Let it marinate in the refrigerator several hours. Serve garnished with mint.

Rice and Parsley Soup
Mako Shark Steaks with Lemon Dill
Green Beans with Sesame Seeds
Sauterne

Serves four

RICE AND PARSLEY SOUP

- 6 tbsp. unsalted butter
- 1 small onion, chopped
- 4 russet potatoes, parboiled for 15 minutes, then grated through the round holes of a grater
- 2 qts. water
- 1 tsp. salt
- ¼ tsp. fresh ground pepper
- Fresh nutmeg
- 4 vegetable or chicken bouillon cubes
- 5 tbsp. chopped parsley
- ¾ cup uncooked rice. Arborio is best, but any white rice is also okay
- 1½ cups Parmesan cheese

Melt 3 tablespoons of the butter. Cook the onion until translucent over medium heat and continue cooking until just starting to turn golden. Then add potatoes, water, salt, pepper, a few grates of nutmeg, bouillon cubes and half of the parsley. Bring slowly to a boil and add rice. Cover and lower heat until rice is just cooked al dente—about 20 minutes. Give one or two quick grinds in food processor if you like. Correct seasoning. Add cheese and remaining butter and parsley.

MAKO SHARK STEAKS WITH LEMON DILL BUTTER

- 1½ sticks of unsalted butter at room temperature
- 2 tsp. dried dill, revived in a little hot water
- 1 tsp. lemon juice
- 1 tsp. grated lemon rind
- Pinch of cayenne pepper

Salt and pepper
4 good-sized shark steaks, 1-inch thick
Flour for dusting

In advance, whip 1 stick of butter until fluffy. Add the dill, lemon juice, lemon zest, cayenne, salt and pepper. Whip until well mixed and then turn out onto plastic wrap and roll up like a small log. Freeze for 24 hours. Bring to refrigerator a few hours before using.

Dry steaks with paper towels. Season lightly with salt and pepper and dust lightly with flour, shaking off excess. Heat remaining 4 tablespoons of unseasoned butter over medium high heat until sizzling. Add steaks and cook 8 minutes first side and 6 to 8 minutes the second side. They should be nice and golden brown. Place on warm plates or platter and top with ½-inch slices of the compound butter. Let sit a few seconds so the butter starts to melt before serving or run under the broiler.

GREEN BEANS WITH SESAME SEEDS

1½ lbs. green beans, ends removed (If beans are quite long, cut in half on the diagonal.)
1½ tbsp. sesame seeds
3-4 tbsp. unsalted butter
Salt and pepper

Blanch the beans until al dente in a large quantity of boiling salted water. Refresh in ice water and drain. This may be done several hours before serving time and then wrap the beans in a dish towel and refrigerate. Toast sesame seeds on medium heat in a heavy skillet. Just as they start to turn a golden color remove from the heat and transfer to a plate or bowl. Just before serving time, melt the butter until hot. Sauté the beans, stirring until heated through. Add sesame seeds, season with salt and pepper. Toss and serve.

Capered Dolphin
Red, Green and Yellow Pepper Salad
Sweet Pastry with Jam

Serves four

CAPERED DOLPHIN

- 1½ sticks unsalted butter
- Salt and pepper
- 1 large clove garlic, chopped
- 1 tsp. grated lemon rind
- 1½ tbsp. chopped capers (the big ones are best), well rinsed first if salted
- 1 tsp. finely chopped parsley
- 1½-2 lbs. dolphin fillets

In advance make the compound butter. Whip the butter until light and fluffy. Add salt and pepper, garlic, lemon zest, capers and parsley. Mix well and mound onto plastic wrap. Form into a cylinder and freeze for 24 hours. Bring to room temperature before using.

Broil the dolphin for about 10 minutes (depending on thickness of steaks) and put a little of the caper butter on top about two-thirds of the way through the cooking.

RED, GREEN, AND YELLOW PEPPER SALAD

- 3 large peppers of each color, cored, seeded, julienned and the red peppers kept separate from the yellow and green
- 3 tbsp. corn oil
- Salt and pepper
- ⅓ cup red wine vinegar or balsamic vinegar
- 1 tsp. prepared mustard
- 2 shallots, chopped very fine
- 1 tbsp. dried tarragon, revived in a little hot water
- ⅔ cup good olive oil, added last

Sauté peppers, yellow and green together, red separately, in corn oil until just al dente. Season with salt and pepper. Blend the remaining ingredients well to make the dressing. Toss peppers altogether with the dressing and serve at room temperature.

SWEET PASTRY WITH JAM

- ½ cup unsalted butter softened
- ⅓ cup sugar
- Pinch of salt
- 1 tsp. grated lemon rind
- 2-3 eggs
- 1 cup all-purpose flour
- ½ cup corn flour
- 1 tsp. baking powder
- 1 jar of jam

Cream butter and add sugar, salt, lemon zest and 1 egg. Mix well. Mix both flours and the baking powder together and add to the butter mixture by flattening it against the side of the bowl with a large spatula, sort of squeezing it into the butter and sugar and then flatten and shape into a disk shape. Wrap dough in plastic wrap and chill for several hours. Using a piece of plastic wrap to cover it, roll out the dough to ¼- to ⅜-inch thickness on a floured piece of parchment paper. Chill for half hour, then remove from the fridge and using a cookie cutter cut 3 to 4-inch ovals, squares, etc. Gather scraps and reroll to get as many cookies as possible. Beat the two remaining eggs and paint the surface of each piece with a thin layer of beaten egg. Spoon a tablespoon or so of jam (apricot or raspberry jam are good classics, but try fig, marmalade, etc.) in the center of the dough. Fold it over and seal by pushing down with the tines of a fork around the edges excluding the folded edge. Now paint the tops with beaten egg. Place cookies on buttered baking sheets. Bake in preheated 350° oven until golden, about 20 minutes. Cool on racks. You will be surprised how many of these little delectables people can eat.

Piña Coladas
Banana Chips
Wahoo Steaks Shish Kebab
White Rice
Grilled Pineapple with Orange Ice

Serves four

See page 95 for Banana Chips recipe. You know how to make white rice.

WAHOO STEAKS SHISH KEBAB

- 1½ tbsp. dried oregano, reconstituted
- ⅔ cup olive oil
- Juice of 1 lemon
- A pinch each of salt and pepper
- ¼ tsp. chopped garlic
- 4 good-sized steaks, 1½-inch thick, cut into squares
- 1 green pepper, cut in large pieces
- 2 sweet red peppers, cut in large pieces
- 1 large sweet onion, cubed
- 12 firm cherry tomatoes

Combine oregano, oil, lemon juice, salt, pepper and garlic and marinate fish cubes for several hours. Assemble shish kebabs, putting cherry tomatoes on last. Grill, turning once. Paint with marinade; serve with white rice. Also, these steaks may be served with any of the compound butter sauces listed with other firm-fleshed fish steaks.

GRILLED PINEAPPLE WITH ORANGE ICE

1 fresh pineapple skinned, cored and cut into 1-inch slices
Sprinkles of Grand Marnier
1 pint orange ice

Sprinkle the pineapple slices with Grand Marnier and grill quickly until hot and slightly browned. Place slices on a plate and top each with a scoop of orange ice.

Fish From the Tropics

I'm lucky enough to have fished now quite a few times in tropical places. Often my catch is small, catching perhaps one fish in a day, maybe none. I'm not sorry for that.

There was the time in Jamaica with Ed and Patrick and Marcie when we went up the Black River looking for tarpon and saw a massive swirl created by a very large tail but nothing more. There was the time in Tortola when a friend of mine threw his fishing gear, tackle bag and all, into a wave on an outgoing tide. Frustration, I guess, at the wiliness of the fish. There was the time when I was twelve out in front of my grandparents' house on the Gulf of Mexico with my brother and sister and grandfather when even shrimp wouldn't catch them. And then, more recently, on Green Turtle Cay, when it was so windy fly casting was more about just getting the fly out there than catching a fish.

But I've never really been sorry about coming up short in those places. Since my first time saltwater fishing, at about the age of eight, I found other things to think about than the catching. I remember standing on some coral rocks casting out to sea at dusk and cranking back, forever casting and cranking, casting and cranking with the odd tug here or nibble there. What was that! I'd follow the line down to where it disappeared into the water and think about the bait (later it would be a plug or fly) dancing along flashing in front of fish, lots of fish, and fantasize about what would finally grab the hook. The fantasy played on, so fancifully and with such great mystery that I think I forgot that I wasn't catching fish. And I'm sure I was just as happy for it—well, nearly just as happy. Many times since, my mind has made that trip to the tropical fantasy world (we refer to it as our brains taking a trip to the Bahamas) while fishing—and okay, sometimes while not.

And although I can think of no tastier fish to eat than pompano or snapper, I just sometimes prefer the slow, sweet, magical tropics with no fish to eat—just wonderful, fanciful memories to store.

But in case you must come back to reality, these menus will help.

Grilled Pompano with Mint and Orange Rind
Brown Rice with Pignoli Nuts and Green Beans
Your Nice Green Salad
Sauterne and Sugar Cookies

Serves four

Pignoli nuts, or pine nuts as they are also called, are a perfectly wonderful nut to add to boring vegetables and should probably be kept on hand at all times. My cooking teacher, Cintra, demanded that all nuts be cooked (roasted or sautéed) if they are used in a recipe. This is a common demand of real cooks. A word of caution: Pignoli nuts burn quite easily if you try to roast them. I find dry sautéing them in a fry pan easier to handle—stirring the nuts and shaking the pan as you cook them—and a better way to avoid the risk of burning these expensive little nuts.

Serve a mild green salad with no bitter greens and sauterne and sugar cookies for dessert. (See page 35 for cookie recipe.)

GRILLED POMPANO WITH MINT AND ORANGE RIND

2 tbsp. dried mint, revived
1½ sticks unsalted butter
   Salt and fresh ground pepper to taste
   Grated rind of 1 orange
   Dash of Tabasco sauce
1 lb. pompano fillets, skin removed

Reconstitute the mint in warm water. Whip the butter until light and fluffy. Add salt and pepper, orange zest, Tabasco and mint. Mix well and mound onto plastic wrap. Form into a cylinder and freeze for 24 hours. Bring to room temperature before using. Grill the pompano a few minutes on each side.

Just before done, put a few pats of the butter on the fish and add some more after it's cooked.

BROWN RICE WITH PIGNOLI NUTS AND GREEN BEANS

 2¼ cups water
 1 tbsp. salt
 1 cup brown rice
 ¼ cup pignoli nuts
 ½ lb. green beans, blanched
  Salt, pepper
 2 tbsp. noisette butter or to taste

Bring water to a boil and add the salt and rice. Cover and reduce heat and cook until tender, about 30 to 45 minutes. Dry sauté the pignoli nuts until golden brown. Mix together the rice and nuts and add the green beans which you've cut on the diagonal into ½-inch pieces and blanched for 1 minute. Add salt and pepper and a little noisette butter, about 2 to 3 tablespoons. (This is melted butter allowed to continue to cook until it turns hazelnut in color.)

Grilled Red Snapper with Lime Butter Sauce and Grilled Pineapple
Bibb Salad
Cornbread
Coconut Ice Cream

Serves four

Ice cream is very satisfying to make at home even if you live where it is very easy to get fresh, local ice cream. I don't think it is worthwhile to either crank by hand or spend a lot of money on a fancy ice cream maker. The extremes are unnecessary. Just buy a $30 electric machine; that will do the job nicely.

GRILLED RED SNAPPER WITH LIME BUTTER SAUCE AND GRILLED PINEAPPLE

- 1 lime
- 2 tbsp. vinegar
- ¼ cup white wine
- Salt and pepper
- 2 shallots, chopped fine and sautéed in butter
- 8 oz. plus a tbsp. (for sautéing the shallots) unsalted butter
- 4 fillets of red snapper
- 8 very thin slices of pineapple, peeled and cored

Peel the rind of one lime with potato peeler, being sure to remove only the green rind and none of the white pith. Cut into pieces the size of matchsticks and blanch in boiling water for 2 minutes.

Combine the vinegar, wine, salt and pepper with the cooked shallots and reduce by half to two-thirds. Now with the vinegar wine reduction at a hot but not boiling temperature, add the butter in small bits, whisking constantly. The sauce will become foamy and white. Paint the fish and the pineapple lightly with the butter sauce. Put the pineapple on the grill a little before the fish. You will want it chewy and lightly caramelized. Grill fish until done. Put the remaining butter sauce under the fish on the plate with the pineapple around. Sprinkle a little of the lime rind on top.

BIBB SALAD

- 2 tbsp. red wine vinegar
- ½ cup good olive oil
- 1 tsp. prepared mustard
- Salt and pepper
- 4 heads Bibb lettuce, cleaned
- A few snips of chive

Combine vinegar, oil, mustard, and salt and pepper in a blender and zip on high for a second or two. Toss with the lettuce and chives.

CORNBREAD

- 1½ cups cornmeal
- 2 tsp, baking powder
- 1 tsp. salt
- 2 tbsp. sugar
- ¼ cup flour
- 1 tbsp. finely diced sweet red pepper
- 3 tbsp. bacon drippings
- 2 eggs
- 1 cup buttermilk
- Butter for greasing the pan

Sift together the cornmeal, baking powder, salt, sugar and flour. Sauté the red pepper in the bacon fat. Beat the eggs, add the buttermilk and red pepper along with the bacon drippings. Now combine this with the dry ingredients. Butter either muffin tins or stick molds and bake in a 425° oven for 15 (stick molds) to 25 (muffin tins) minutes.

COCONUT ICE CREAM

- 2 cups whole milk
- 1 cup granulated sugar
- 1 cup grated coconut
- 6 egg yolks
- 1 cup heavy cream, chilled
- 1 tbsp. coconut liqueur (a coconut flavored rum or white rum)

Bring the milk, ½ cup of the sugar and the coconut to a boil. Just as it boils, remove from the heat. Cover pot and let rest until cool.

Combine the egg yolks and the other ½ cup sugar and mix with whisk or electric beater until thick and creamy. Add the cooled coconut milk to the egg yolk mixture. Mix well. Return to heat in heavy-bottomed saucepan, and over medium heat stirring constantly, cook until it thickens, which it will do quite suddenly (between 5 to 10 minutes). Pour into a large bowl and stir for a few minutes to stop cooking. Add the heavy cream, the liqueur and stir well to mix. Chill mixture well, stirring from time to time, for 3 to 6 hours. Make according to your ice cream machine's directions. Serve with chocolate cookies.

Saltwater Bottom Fish

When I first wrote this book in 1986 all three fish in this chapter were so plentiful in numbers that they were relatively easy to catch, intentionally or unintentionally, and consequently considered rather ho-hum for the sport fisherman. Although population levels remain high for flounder and sea bass (not to be confused with the Chilean sea bass), sadly cod is now a much depleted resource worldwide. But cod is still very catch-able and since all three are delightfully flavored fish, actually true culinary stars, and taste best when absolutely fresh—as fresh as only a fisherman gets them—then it's important to focus on them from the cook's vantage.

And although the menus listed here for cod, flounder and sea bass are well suited to them, any, yes any, of the other fish recipes will work. Rarely is there a recipe in this book that will not work well on some species of fish other than the one it calls for. A recipe for a nice delicate brook trout will work well also on smallmouth bass. Went out for striper and came home with weakfish? Use the same recipe you were planning for striper on the weakfish. I have tried to group the fish by chapters according to likeness, not only likeness of habitat and species characteristics but also according to what recipes will work equally as well on all species within that chapter. In mixing species and menus be concerned mostly with matching the proper cooking technique to the size or cut of fish. Grilling a flounder fillet would be nearly impossible, the fillets so tiny they'd end up slipping through the grate onto the coals. (But as you'll see in the first recipe below, there is a trick...) Thoughtful improvisation in the kitchen is very similar to matching the hatch on the river and can breed the same success and feeling of satisfaction. So go for it, mix and match your fish and recipes with wild abandon!

Chinese Grilled Flounder with Noodles
Sautéed Watercress
Pear Sorbet with Fortune Cookies

Serves four

Sautéing greens was a revelation to me. Not only can it be done with watercress, but spinach and parsley. It's very tasty and easy and solves that age-old problem of what to do with the remaining bunch after you've used the three sprigs for garnish.

CHINESE GRILLED FLOUNDER WITH NOODLES

¼ cup canola oil
1 tbsp. lemon juice
2 tbsp. soy sauce
1 tbsp. rice wine vinegar
1 large garlic clove, chopped fine
1 piece ginger, peeled, chopped fine
1 shake red pepper flakes
1½ lbs. flounder, skinned and trimmed
1 lb. oriental pasta
1 lb. mushrooms
1 tbsp. sesame oil
¼ cup peanuts or cashews, toasted in corn oil and coarsely chopped
3-6 scallions, green part only, cut into 1-inch pieces
Salt and pepper

Blend the oil, lemon juice, soy sauce, vinegar, garlic, ginger, and red pepper flakes in a blender, adding the canola oil last. Pour over fish, let rest several hours. Wrap the fish with the juices in foil and grill on a preheated grill, 2 to 3 minutes per side. Cook and drain the pasta and place the fish on top of it. Sauté the mushrooms quickly in the sesame oil. Remove from the heat and add the nuts and scallions. Season with salt and pepper. Top the fish with the nut and mushroom mixture and any leftover marinade.

SAUTÉED WATERCRESS

3 bunches watercress
3 tbsp. unsalted butter
  Salt and pepper

Wash and spin dry each bunch of watercress and cut into 2-inch lengths (the bunches should be cut approximately into thirds). Sauté the watercress in the hot unsalted butter for a second or two and then add the lid for two minutes. Remove the lid, season with salt and pepper and a little more butter and serve.

PEAR SORBET

1 cup sugar
1 cup water
1 qt. ripe pears peeled, cored and puréed
2 tbsp. lemon juice
  A pinch of salt
1 tbsp. pear liqueur

Boil the sugar and water together for 5 minutes. To the puréed pears add sugar syrup to taste, lemon juice to taste, a pinch of salt, and pear liqueur. Chill mixture for 3 to 6 hours, and then freeze according to your ice cream machine's directions. Serve with fortune cookies.

Gray Flounder
Sautéed Spinach
Fried Bread

Serves four

GRAY FLOUNDER

- 2 large carrots or 8 tiny ones, julienned
- 3 sticks celery, julienned
- 1 potato, julienned
- 1 tbsp. orange rind, julienned and blanched for 30 seconds
- 1 tsp. garlic, finely minced
- 2 tbsp. unsalted butter
- 4 flounder fillets
- 1½ cups heavy cream
- 1 tbsp. clam juice
- Salt and pepper

Sauté the vegetables, orange rind and garlic in the butter until just barely tender. Set aside. In a stove-to-table container, set some vegetables, about half, on the bottom of the dish. Arrange fish on top. Reduce the cream by boiling it in a frying pan until it is halved, then add the clam juice to the cream and whisk. Pour over the fish. Add the remaining vegetables on top of the fish criss-cross or put in little bunches if you wish. Cook at a simmer uncovered for about 5 minutes. Season fish with salt and pepper and serve on heated plates.

SAUTÉED SPINACH

    1 lb. spinach
    2 tbsp. unsalted butter
       Fresh grated nutmeg
       Salt and pepper

Rinse and spin dry spinach. Remove stems and sauté in butter until just wilted. Season with a few grates of fresh nutmeg, salt, and pepper.

FRIED BREAD

    8 1-inch slices of French or Italian bread
    4 tbsp. unsalted butter
       Salt and pepper
    2 tbsp. fontina cheese, grated, or any cheese

Dry bread in oven at 300°. Fry in melted butter. Sprinkle with salt and pepper and cheese. Put back in oven to just melt the cheese.

Flounder and Scallop Soup
Fried Bread
Fig Tart

Serves four

If you cannot get the small bay or Cape scallops or have caught an extraordinary number of flounder, just use all flounder in this recipe. The recipe for Fried Bread can be found on page 117.

FLOUNDER AND SCALLOP SOUP

For the fumet (stock) of fish:
- 1 medium onion, chopped into pieces
- 1 very small carrot, sliced
- A few mushrooms
- 4 parsley stems
- 3 tbsp. unsalted butter
- 3-4 lbs. fish bones, preferably sole and flounder, heads included. Just remove the triangle of innards.
- 3 cups of very good white wine
- 5 cups water
- Large pinch salt
- Pinch thyme
- 1 small bay leaf
- 10 peppercorns

This recipe will make about two quarts of stock. Please do not use an aluminum pot to make it in and please remember the better the wine, the better the soup. And with a nice fish stock you can put almost anything in the soup.

Cook the onion, carrot, mushrooms and parsley stems in butter for 5 to 8 minutes. Add fish bones, cover pot, and let stew over low heat for a while until fish bones sort of collapse—about 10 minutes. Remove the lid and then add wine and 5 cups water. Bring to a boil and add salt, thyme, bay leaf and peppercorns. On medium heat, simmer for 30 minutes. Strain immediately. It should smell delicious and may be made a day ahead.

For the soup:
- 1 pint scallops, sliced if necessary
- 2-3 fillets of flounder, chopped to bite-size pieces
- 2 small zucchinis, julienned into matchstick size pieces, blanched
- 2 small yellow squash, julienned into matchstick size pieces, blanched
- 1 cup small broccoli florets, blanched
- Salt and pepper

Taste fish stock and heat. Add scallops and cook for a few minutes until almost done. Add fish and vegetables. Cook for a few minutes more and season to taste and serve immediately. (A red wine fumet is also nice if using salmon or stronger types of fish.)

FIG TART

- ½ cup rum
- 2 tbsp. honey
- 2 tbsp. unsalted butter, plus some for pans
- 18 green figs
- 1 recipe pastry (yours or mine p. 219) or Pepperidge Farm puff pastry
- Sugar
- 1 cup heavy cream
- 2 tsp. confectioners' sugar

Cook together the rum, honey and butter. Place figs in buttered dish and baste with the rum mixture. Cook at 350° until soft, but not too soft. The cooking time will vary depending on how ripe they are. Let cool. Roll out and line a buttered tart pan with pastry. Let sit 1 hour in the fridge. Preheat oven to 425° for 20 minutes. Line pastry with tin foil and fill with beans or rice. Cook 5 to 7 minutes until set. Remove tin foil filled with beans and sprinkle tart with granulated sugar. Continue to cook until the sugar starts to caramelize. Remove from oven and slip out of pan onto cooling rack. This can be done several hours ahead. Whip the cream with the confectioners' sugar. Add a little dash of rum if you like and spread on pastry. Arrange figs on top and brush with any leftover liquid. Serve within 1 hour.

Fish Chowder
Common Crackers
Green Salad
Gingerbread

Serves four

Cod is a wonderful fish if it is eaten very fresh; some people prefer it to haddock. Most of the recipes in this book would be appropriate to try on cod, but if you do not have a fresh cod or you had to freeze the fish this recipe is perfect to use.

FISH CHOWDER

½ amount of potatoes as fish, peeled
½ lb. unsalted butter
1 8-lb. cod (approximately), cleaned and cut up
  Salt and pepper
  Pinch thyme
1 7.5 oz. can evaporated milk
½ pint all-purpose cream
1 qt. milk (approximately)
  Salted pork
  Crackers

Slice potatoes and put in kettle with some of the butter, about 4 tablespoons, and a little water to cover. Bring to a boil and simmer about 10 minutes. Add cut up fish and salt and pepper to taste. Add more water to cover and a pinch of thyme and cook 30 minutes or until fish is tender. Stir in remaining butter and evaporated milk and cream. Add regular milk to obtain the fluid level you want. Taste for seasoning. Let simmer, but do not let boil again. Serve with fried salted pork and common crackers.

GINGERBREAD

- ½ cup unsalted butter, softened, plus some for buttering pan
- ⅔ cup light brown sugar
- 1 egg
- 1½ cups all-purpose flour, plus some for dusting pan
- 1 ¼ tsp. ground ginger
- 1 tsp. ground cinnamon
- ¾ tsp. ground cloves
- 1 tsp, baking soda
- ½ cup unsulphured molasses
- ½ cup boiling water
- Confectioners' sugar
- 1 cup heavy cream
- Dash of rum

Preheat the oven to 350°. Butter a 13 by 9 by 2-inch baking pan. Put a piece of parchment paper on the bottom of the buttered pan and butter that and dust with flour.

Whip butter until fluffy. Add brown sugar and mix well. Add egg and blend well. Sift flour with spices and baking soda and set aside. Combine molasses with boiling water. Alternately add flour/spice mixture and the boiling water/molasses mixture to the butter, sugar, egg mixture until well-combined. Pour batter into prepared baking pan and cook about 25 to 30 minutes or until cake tester comes out clean. Cool in pan on wire rack. Then remove from cake pan. This can be made ahead and stored for several days if tightly wrapped and kept at room temperature. Just before serving, dust with confectioners' sugar. Serve with lightly whipped cream and add a dash of rum to the cream.

Grilled Sea Bass with Sun-Dried Tomatoes, Pepper and Garlic
Straw Potato-Corn Cake
Your Nice Green Salad

Serves four

Sun-dried tomatoes have become more common in recent years and now can be purchased in grocery stores. My own taste dictates the purchase of the more expensive sun-dried tomatoes, the ones packed in olive oil, rather than the ones simply dried, as I like to use the oil in salad dressings and other recipes within the menu to "tie" the tastes together. When you make the vinaigrette for your salad in this menu (see the index or "Basics" chapter, page 217, in this book if you can't think of a good salad on your own) use some of the oil that the sun-dried tomatoes have been packed in.

GRILLED SEA BASS WITH SUN-DRIED TOMATOES, PEPPER AND GARLIC

1 3-pound sea bass, butterflied (scaled, skin left on, head and tail removed, then boned and split)
Salt and pepper
1 sprig fresh basil or 1 tsp. dried
1 sprig fresh thyme or 1 tsp. dried
1 small onion, sliced finely
½ cup olive oil
2 cloves garlic, minced
1 large green pepper, cored and chopped into ½-inch pieces
½ cup sun-dried tomatoes in oil, roughly chopped
Handful of parsley

(If the sun-dried tomatoes are not in oil: in a small pot add the tomatoes, 1 cup olive oil, 1 small clove garlic and a pinch thyme. Heat until hot and keep warm for 20 minutes or until tomatoes have plumped. Drain off oil and reserve for another use. It's great in salads.)

Dry fish and season with salt and pepper. Stuff with basil and thyme. Wrap tightly in foil and refrigerate for 2 to 4 hours. Preheat grill. Do not remove foil and cook 15 minutes one side and 12 the other. Test for doneness. While the fish is cooking or ahead of time make the sauce: Sauté onion in olive oil over medium-low heat until translucent. Add garlic, peppers and tomatoes. Cook until peppers are done to taste. Season with salt and pepper and a handful of chopped parsley. Let sit 20 minutes at least to meld flavors. Remove the herbs from the fish and spoon the sauce over it. Serve with a green salad.

STRAW POTATO-CORN CAKE

    1½ lbs. baking potatoes
    4 tbsp. unsalted butter
    2 tbsp. oil
    6 tbsp. creamed corn
      Salt and pepper

Peel potatoes, cut into ⅛-inch slices and then into ⅛-inch matchstick strips, or easier still, cut into matchstick juliennes in your food processor. In a 10-inch, non-stick pan heat half the butter and all the oil until hot and add half the potatoes and spread around the center on top of the potatoes about 6 tablespoons cold creamed corn. Season with salt and pepper. Then add the rest of the potatoes. Season with salt and pepper and press down with spatula. Cook until the bottom is browned, by which time the whole cake will move as one. (Be sure you squish those potatoes down occasionally.) When the bottom is golden brown, cover and lower the heat, cook 7 minutes or until the center of the cake is done. Remove cover and raise the heat. Flip the potato cake over and add remaining butter and oil and brown the other side.

HONEY ICE CREAM

⅓ cup very aromatic and high quality honey
2 cups milk
6 egg yolks
⅔ cup sugar
1 cup heavy cream, chilled
  Crystallized lavender flowers for decoration
  (These can be purchased at a gourmet shop.)

Bring honey and milk slowly to the scalding point while stirring. Remove from heat and cool, stirring occasionally. Mix egg yolks and sugar together and beat until a light ribbon is formed. The mixture will be thick and creamy. Combine egg-sugar together with the milk-honey, whisking just to mix. Using a heavy-bottomed saucepan, return to medium-high heat and stir constantly until the mixture thickens. Remove immediately from the heat and pour through a fine strainer into a large bowl and cool, stirring occasionally. Add heavy cream and mix well. Chill mixture thoroughly, about 3 to 6 hours. Make ice cream according to your ice cream machine's instructions. Serve garnished with crystallized violets.

Tautog with Asparagus and Vegetables
Your Favorite Salad
Fried Bread
Fresh Fruit
Cheeses

Serves four

In recent years, there seems to be a tendency in folks to not automatically eat dessert. Perhaps this is because we've all become more concerned about calories and sugar intake in general, but maybe we never really craved sugar that much anyway. Maybe cooks just kept thrusting desserts on us automatically because desserts are fun to cook and supposedly complement the meal. I've tried to stay away from heavy desserts in this book because they don't really suit fish and seem actually to contradict the idea of a light, low-calorie main course. Fruit is a perfect dessert if you truly must have a sweet after fish. See the "Basics" chapter, page 222 or index for suggestions on salads if you don't have your own favorite. The recipe for Fried Bread can be found on page 117.

TAUTOG WITH ASPARAGUS AND VEGETABLES

- 2 medium carrots cut into a 2 by ¼-inch julienne
- 1 celery stalk, cut into 2 by ¼-inch julienne
- 1 leek, white part only, cut into 2 by ¼-inch julienne
- 2 tbsp. unsalted butter
- ½ cup fish stock, or mild chicken stock, or if neither then just plain water
- Pinch of salt
- 1½ cups heavy cream
- 2 lbs. tautog (or also known as blackfish) fillets
- Salt and pepper
- 1 lb. asparagus, cut into 2-inch pieces, peeled, blanched, refreshed in ice water and drained
- 2 Idaho potatoes, cooked, peeled and quartered
- 1 tomato, peeled, seeded and coarsely chopped and set aside
- 1 tbsp. chopped chives

In heavy-bottomed cooking pot, sauté carrots, celery, and leek for 3 minutes in ½ tablespoon hot butter. Add hot stock or water and a pinch of salt. Stir, cover for a few minutes and then remove cover to let most of the liquid evaporate. Any liquid left when the vegetables are cooked but crisp, add to the cream. Set vegetables aside. Pour cream into cooking casserole. Add the fish, a little salt and pepper and bring to a low simmer. Cook uncovered for 2 minutes and then drain off the cream and reserve. Add the carrots, leeks, celery, and asparagus to the fish. Add one potato to the cream. Put potato and cream in a food processor and blend only briefly (so as not to whip the cream). Add the rest of the potato. Blend again. Add 1 tablespoon plus 1 teaspoon butter, and season with salt and pepper. Pour this over fish and vegetables. Bring to a full boil. Remove from heat. Add tomato and chives and serve in heated soup plates with Fried Bread (page 217).

Stir-fry Snow Peas with Broccoli
Black Sea Bass Chinese Style
White Rice
Fortune Cookies

Serves four

I thought you would know how to cook white rice so I did not include a recipe for it. Also, I have found that rice lovers all have their own very definite ideas as to what brand, converted or not, sticky or dry the rice should be. Fortune cookies need to be bought.

STIR-FRY SNOW PEAS WITH BROCCOLI

- 1 head of broccoli
- 2 tbsp. sesame oil
- 2 tbsp. unsalted butter
- 1 lb. snow peas, ends and strings removed
-   Salt and pepper

Remove bite-size florets from the broccoli and blanch. Heat the oil and butter together and add the snow peas and florets. Stir constantly and till hot and season with salt and pepper.

BLACK SEA BASS CHINESE STYLE

- 3 lbs. of black sea bass, the average size is 1-3 lbs, so 2 smaller or 1 bigger
- 2 tbsp. dry sherry
- ¼ cup plus 2 tsp. soy sauce
- Pepper
- 3 tbsp. corn oil
- 2 tbsp. sesame oil
- 4 tbsp. peeled and julienned ginger
- 5 scallions, white and green parts cleaned, in 1-inch pieces
- 1 clove garlic, chopped fine
- ½ cup water
- 1 tsp. sugar
- The juices from the cooked fish
- Salt and pepper

Bone, clean, wash and dry the fish and leave head and tail on. Score the fish on both sides and lay it on a large piece of foil. Combine the sherry and 2 teaspoons of soy sauce to make a basting liquid. Sprinkle the fish with the liquid and a grind of pepper and fold up carefully to encase all liquid. Steam over boiling water in steamer for 15 minutes. Meanwhile, in heavy saucepan, heat the two oils until hot. Lower heat and add ginger. Cook 1 to 2 minutes. Add scallions, garlic and cook 20 seconds. Add ¼ cup soy sauce, water, sugar. Stir well and set aside. Remove fish from foil as soon as cooked. Save juices. If a lot, reduce to 5 to 6 tablespoons. Add to sauce. Season with salt and pepper. Pour over fish. Serve on a decorative platter.

Shellfish

In a fish cookbook that is written for fishermen, you may ask why I include a chapter about shellfish: Don't you know shellfish aren't fish and can't sportingly be caught with rod and line, dummy? The reason has to do with philosophy.

Knowles was a great fisherman. Ted Williams wrote about him several times in *Gray's Sporting Journal* and Knowles truly became a legend in his own time. This is partially because he was such a humorous character, and because he was old and had seen a lot, and because it's human nature to make old people legends. But we do all know, particularly in the hunting and fishing part of our lives, good and interesting characters who are old. Knowles did go beyond that.

Years ago now we used to go to Nantucket for the fish-all-night, sleep-all-day ritual of attempting to catch striped bass. They were long, hard nights trudging around in heavy waders, casting in the waist-high surf, travelling up and down the long beaches in four-wheel-drive vehicles looking for the then dwindling populace of striped bass. There was a gamut of emotions in this fishing: beautiful sunrises, but visions of Jaws lurking in inky-black waters; cold winds and jovial jeep-side conversation, all to end with daybreak and falling exhausted into bed. Except for Knowles, who went to play golf. He'd been there on the beaches in his Willys catching more fish than anyone else, but for some reason he wasn't ever tired the next day. I kept imagining him as a three-year-old: his mother must have gone 'round the bend trying to keep up with him. Even when Knowles couldn't find someone to play golf with, he didn't sleep, he just went somewhere.

I'd fished with Knowles, I'd drunk whisky with Knowles at 7:00 in the morning, so it was time to travel with Knowles through the day that came after a sleepless night. He drove me all over the island in his Willys, not to the town of Nantucket or to Siasconset or to the places the tourists saw or to places I'd ever seen before. Just to the places that were beautiful. And he knew the name of every tree, every bird, every flower that we saw. He stopped at last in front of a saltwater pond; you could see the ocean on the other side of the dunes. There was a mound of shells, all one kind, all white, as high as I was. Beautiful scallop shells and he stared at them in wonderment. For just as Knowles will watch the birds to figure where to fish, he will find the hills of shells to find the scallop beds. Watching and concentrating on nature is it.

The happiness derived from fishing is similar to that derived from collecting mussels or trapping lobsters. We observe and learn about nature in order to gather selectively from it, and to eat what is best from it. It is the same philosophy and attitude whether it's a fisherman's or a scalloper's.

Oyster Stew
Grits
Your Own Nice Green Salad
Apple Tart

Serves four

In my mind, for many years, I likened grits to oatmeal. They were gloppy and ugly and eaten not because they tasted good but because you wanted to stay warm or get warm or add bulk to your meal. This is still true in my mind about oatmeal but the image has completely changed when it comes to grits. Grits are absolutely delicious and Northerners should make more of an effort to incorporate them into their menus. There is still one similarity between grits and oatmeal: It's a good idea to add a lot of flavoring to the grits, like butter or cheese or cayenne. I also think it's a good idea to stay away from the quick cooking or instant grits. They're simply not as tasty.

OYSTER STEW

- 1 pint shucked oysters with their liquid
- 2 large shallots
- 1-2 tbsp. unsalted butter
- 3 cups light cream or mixture of heavy cream and milk
- Salt and pepper
- Tiny pinch tarragon

Drain oysters in a strainer, catching all liquid. Chop shallots extremely fine and sauté them in butter till translucent but not a bit browned. Add oyster liquid and milk/cream to shallots, salt and pepper and a tiny pinch of tarragon and bring to simmer. Let it sit on a low heat for 5 to 10 minutes and then add the oysters. Heat through to your taste, 2 to 3 minutes and serve.

GRITS

- ¾ cup grits (not quick cooking)
- 3 cups boiling chicken stock—use Knorr chicken cubes or boxed broth, not canned, unless it's College Inn
- 2 eggs
- 2 tsp. salt
- Pepper to taste
- A sprinkle of cayenne pepper
- ½ lb. grated gruyere cheese
- 3 tbsp. unsalted butter

Add grits to boiling stock. Stir over medium-high heat until it bubbles and thickens, about 10 to 15 minutes. Remove from heat. Stir to cool slightly. Add eggs one at a time stirring after each. Season with salt and pepper and cayenne. Now add the cheese. Taste again and add any seasoning. Put in buttered gratin dish with 1 tablespoon of the butter. Dot with remaining butter. Bake for 1 hour. Let sit for a few minutes before serving.

APPLE TART

- 1 recipe pastry, yours or mine (p. 219), or use Pepperidge Farm puff pastry
- 5 Pink Lady apples or your favorite cooking apples
- Cinnamon and sugar
- 2-3 tbsp. unsalted butter
- 1 cup heavy cream
- 1 tbsp. confectioners' sugar
- 1 tbsp. Calvados

Preheat oven to 425°. Roll pastry thin and rectangular in shape. Place on a sheet of lightly floured parchment paper and then slip onto the back side of a large cookie sheet. Let rest 1 hour in the refrigerator. Peel, core and slice apples thin. A ½-inch from the edge of the pastry, arrange apple slices overlapping in any design on pastry. Curl pastry edges to edge of apples. Sprinkle liberally with cinnamon and sugar and dot with butter. Bake till edges of pastry are nicely light brown. Slide onto cooling rack. Check bottom of pastry to see if it's sufficiently browned. Serve hot or cold, with whipped cream with a little confectioners' sugar and some Calvados in it.

Mussels Steamed
Grilled Lamb Chops
Caesar Salad
Fresh Fruit

Serve four

The recipe for Caesar Salad (p. 140) can be used or your choice from the Basics Chapter, (p. 222). And you can choose where and how to grill the lamb chops.

MUSSELS STEAMED

- 1 cups white wine (or enough to cover the bottom of your pot by ½-inch)
- 4 qts. mussels (1 qt. per person)
- 3 tbsp. shallots, finely chopped
- 1 tbsp. unsalted butter
- 3 egg yolks
- 2 cups heavy cream
- Salt and pepper
- Chopped parsley

Bring the wine to a boil. Place the mussels over the wine, not in it, and steam for about 8 to 10 minutes, or until they just pop open. You may need to stir the top mussels down to the bottom so all have an equal opportunity to open. Remove the mussels and pour the wine broth into a large bowl so the sand can settle to the bottom. Sauté the shallots in the butter and then carefully ladle the wine broth into the pan with the shallots. Reduce for a minute or two over a high heat. Meanwhile, in a small bowl beat the egg yolks together with the cream. Now beat in a few tablespoons of the broth. Add the entire egg yolk/cream mixture to the broth and whisk until mixed. Heat till slightly thickened and remove from heat. Add salt and pepper to taste. To serve, divide the mussels into four warmed soup plates and pour the egg broth over. Sprinkle with parsley and serve immediately.

Shrimp Gratin
Simple Green Salad

Serves four

Armagnac is a lesser grade of cognac and is usually cheaper than Courvoisier. I recommend it because you can really splash it on without seeing the dollar signs dribbled all over your shrimp.

SHRIMP GRATIN

- 5 tbsp. unsalted butter, plus some for dotting
- 2 tbsp. flour
- ¼ cup dry white wine
- 1 cup heavy cream reduced with the tarragon to ¾ cup
- 1 tsp. tarragon
- ⅓ cup grated gruyere cheese
- 1 tbsp. mustard
- Salt and pepper and cayenne pepper
- 1 Dash of Armagnac
- 32 medium cooked shrimp or whatever quantity you want for 4 people, or use 4 Maine lobster tails
- ½ cup breadcrumbs

Preheat oven to 325°. Make a light white sauce by combining first the butter, flour, and white wine. Then add to it the reduced cream and tarragon, cheese, mustard, salt, peppers, and Armagnac. Pour over the shrimp. Sprinkle with ½ cup breadcrumbs. Dot with 2 tablespoons butter and cook about 10-15 minutes until hot. Put under broiler until it bubbles, and serve.

Mussel Pizza
Caesar Salad

Serves four

One of the nice aspects of pizza is its versatility. It can be for lunch or dinner or hors d'oeuvres. It can be for children or grown-ups, it can be chic or casual, all depending on what you do with the toppings and what you serve with it. The thinking behind this menu is that it be used for a Sunday night supper with guests. (You can make just one of the pizzas with mussels and use the rest of the dough for a cheese and tomato sauce pizza for the kids.)

MUSSEL PIZZA

For the dough:
- ¾ cup lukewarm water
- ½ tsp. dry yeast
- ½ tsp. honey
- ½ tsp. salt
- 2 cups all-purpose flour
- ¼ cup olive oil

In the bowl of a mix-master fitted with a dough hook, add the warm water, yeast, honey, and salt. Stir and let stand until the yeast looks a little foamy, about 5 minutes. Add in the flour and mix on the "stir" setting. Increase the speed while the flour is still being blended and drizzle in the olive oil and mix until dough is formed. Turn out onto a lightly floured board and knead well for about 5 minutes. The dough will be oily to the touch. Form dough into a ball and place in a plastic bag and let sit overnight, or at least 6 hours, in the refrigerator. Remove the dough from the fridge and divide in half, placing a half on a piece of parchment paper, each about 12 to 14-inches long and dusted with flour. Form each piece of dough into a disk and cover with plastic wrap. Let dough sit 15 minutes before rolling out into thin circles. Slide the parchment paper with each pizza round onto the back of a cookie sheet. Put your toppings on.

For the pizza topping:
- 1 cup white wine
- A few parsley stems
- 1 garlic clove, mashed
- A couple of peppercorns
- 2 qts. mussels, cleaned and de-bearded
- Olive oil
- Lemon juice
- 2 cups shredded mozzarella cheese
- ½ cup finely chopped parsley
- Red pepper flakes

Combine the white wine, parsley stems, garlic, and peppercorns in a large pot. Steam the mussels over the white wine, not in it, till they just start to open and remove immediately. Spread around in one layer on the counter to cool fast. Open and remove mussels to a large bowl and toss with olive oil and lemon juice. (You can also open mussels by placing them in a microwave for a few seconds.)

Put the mozzarella on first, and then add the cooked mussels and sprinkle with parsley, red pepper flakes and olive oil. Bake each pizza one at a time, by again carefully sliding the loaded pizza atop the paper onto a stone in a preheated 500° oven. Bake 8 to 10 minutes or until crust is golden. Slide cooked pizza back onto the cookie sheet and then onto a cutting board to slice. Repeat to cook the second pizza and serve. (If you want to serve just one pizza, roll out both dough disks but put toppings on just one of the rounds. After you've cooked the pizza with toppings and removed it from the oven, slide the second dough round onto the stone and let bake 2 minutes. Remove and freeze. Before using, let defrost 30 minutes before adding toppings. Bake as above.)

CAESAR SALAD

- 1 garlic clove
- ½ cup good quality olive oil
- 1 cup cubed French or Italian bread

- 1½ tsp. salt
- 4-5 Grinds of fresh pepper
- ¼ tsp. dry mustard
- ¼ tsp. Worcestershire sauce
- 3 tbsp. red wine vinegar
- 1 raw egg, lightly beaten
- Juice of 1 lemon, strained
- 2 heads Romaine lettuce, washed and dried
- 4 anchovy fillets, chopped very small
- 3 tbsp. Parmesan cheese, grated

The night before, heat the garlic clove in the olive oil for 15 minutes. Remove from the heat and let sit overnight, and then discard the garlic. Sauté the cubes of bread in 2 tablespoons of the oil and set aside on a plate. Combine the remaining oil, with salt, pepper, Worcestershire sauce, vinegar, egg, and lemon juice. Pour over lettuce and toss very well. Now add the garlic croutons and toss again. Sprinkle the finely chopped anchovy and grated Parmesan over the dressed lettuce. Serve at once.

Egg and Asparagus Salad
Little Shrimp
Baked Apples

Serves four

In 1986 I wrote the following introduction for this shrimp recipe:

> I believe the next stage in the growth and development of our cooking and eating tastes in the United States will be more emphasis on regional foods. We've all been through the fads of French, Northern Italian and Chinese cooking and incorporated into our own style the best of those cuisines. But we are moving now to understanding and appreciating what is locally fresh and uniquely different from the rest of the country or world. This involves not just appreciating the style of Cajun cooking or Southern food, but truly understanding that New Jersey blueberries are different from those grown in Maine or Michigan. One can barely use some of Alice Waters' cookbooks if living outside of California.
>
> To discover your own local treats and invent the cooking methods for them has got to be one of the great delights in cooking. It is also a very good reason to fish. I use this recipe for shrimp on one of our local species which the fishermen call scampi and is available only in the spring. These shrimp are divine. I hope you will find the recipe useful on your shrimp or when you come to New England in the spring.

Now, some twenty-plus years later we are, indeed, seeing a huge emphasis on eating locally. And now that I live in New Hampshire I am unable to get the little scampi shrimp fresh—only frozen. They remain a delightful eating adventure, however, and discovering your own local treats and inventing the cooking methods is truly wonderful. Now in my Northern New England home I get better access to "uncommon" or antique apples then when I lived in Massachusetts. Calville Blanc d'Hiver or Esopus Spitzenberg are my favorite apples for this recipe, but Baldwin or Cortlands work too.

EGG AND ASPARAGUS SALAD

2 hard-boiled eggs
1 tbsp. white vinegar
½ lb. asparagus, peeled
2 heads Boston lettuce, cleaned and dried
1 tbsp. balsamic vinegar
1 tsp. prepared mustard
¼ cup olive oil
 Salt and pepper
1 tbsp. mayonnaise

To hard-boil the eggs, set in cold water with a tablespoon of white vinegar, bring to a boil, reduce to a medium simmer and cook, using a timer, for 9 minutes. Then plunge in cold water. Peel, chop and set aside.

Steam the asparagus, cut into 1-inch pieces and combine with the lettuce. Make a vinaigrette by combining in the blender the balsamic vinegar, mustard, oil and dashes of salt and pepper and blending for a second or two. Add the mayonnaise and motorize for another second. Toss the vinaigrette first with the asparagus and lettuce and then add chopped egg. Toss lightly, taste for salt and pepper and serve.

LITTLE SHRIMP

2½ lbs. tiny shrimp
4 tbsp. unsalted butter
2 tbsp. Armagnac
1 cup heavy cream
 Salt and freshly ground pepper

The tiny shrimp from Maine or the little San Francisco Bay shrimp are superb. You cook them whole, heads and tails and then shell and eat at the table. It's very messy but worth it at least once a year.

Clean the shrimp of debris. Try not to wash too much unless they are gritty. In a large frying pan over medium high heat cook butter stirring until it is a light brown color. Add shrimp instantly and cook on high heat shaking or stirring until shells turn red. Remove from heat and cover pan for about 5 minutes. This will finish the cooking. With a slotted spoon scoop out shrimp to a platter. Return pan to high heat and add Armagnac. Let bubble a little and then add cream and cook until reduced by half. Taste for seasoning and add salt and pepper as necessary. Add shrimp and oozed out liquid to the pan and reheat. Taste for seasoning again and serve immediately with French bread to mop up the sauce. Remove the head, pull off the shell and what a delicious treat!

BAKED APPLES

- 4 large apples, cored and with their tops cut off
- 4 tbsp. marmalade
- 4 tsp. raisins
- 1 stick unsalted butter
- 1 store-bought yellow (pound or Génoise) cake
- 1½ cups heavy cream
- 1 tbsp. confectioners' sugar
- 1½ tbsp. Grand Marnier liqueur

Stuff the opening in each apple with marmalade and raisins. Dot with half of the butter and bake at 325° for approximately 40 minutes. While the apples are cooking, fry 4 slices, about an inch thick, of yellow cake in remaining 4 tablespoons unsalted butter. Combine and whip lightly the cream, sugar and Grand Marnier. To serve, set each apple on a slice of cake. Pour cooking juices around and pass on the side the lightly whipped cream.

Lobster with Anchovy Garlic Butter
Tomato Bread
Your Simplest Green Salad
Drunk Melons

Serves four

Your salad is good here or refer to the index or "Basics" chapter in this book (p. 222) for suggestions.

LOBSTER WITH ANCHOVY GARLIC BUTTER

For the anchovy garlic butter:

- 1½ sticks unsalted butter, softened
- 2 medium cloves garlic-mashed with the side of a knife and then chopped fine
- 1 anchovy fillet, chopped fine
- Salt and pepper
- A squeeze of lemon juice

Make in advance. Whip the butter until fluffy. Add the remaining ingredients and whip again. Place onto plastic wrap and mold into a log shape. Freeze for at least 24 hours and then bring into the refrigerator about an hour before it is to be used.

For the lobsters:

- 4 1-lb. lobsters
- 1 cup good olive oil
- 8 peeled garlic cloves
- 1½ tsp. dried thyme
- 1 bay leaf

Kill the lobsters by submerging in boiling water for a minute, or do so by inserting a sharp knife just where the head joins the shell to cut the spinal cord. Then turn the lobster over and cut carefully through the cartilage, down the length of the body. Open it out, (save coral and tamale) and crack the claws. Heat on low heat the oil, garlic, thyme, and bay leaf for 20-30 minutes. Remove garlic and bay leaf and keep the garlic for whatever sounds good. Brush the lobsters with the oil and grill flesh side down 7 minutes. Turn and put a dollop of the anchovy garlic butter on and cook for another 2 minutes. The lobsters are cooked when the flesh is just opaque.

TOMATO BREAD

- 8 ½-inch slices French or Italian bread or a good country whole wheat
- 4 ripe good (they must be very good) tomatoes, peeled, seeded and coarsely chopped
- Pinch of basil
- ½ cup olive oil (approximately)
- Salt and pepper

On cookie sheet bake the bread at 300° until just light golden. Cook the tomatoes in 1 tablespoon of the olive oil and the pinch of basil over medium heat until most of the liquid has evaporated and the tomatoes start to mush together. Cool. Spread a very small amount over each slice of bread and drizzle with olive oil. Sprinkle with salt and pepper and serve at once.

DRUNK MELONS

- 2 very ripe melons (they may be of 2 different varieties)
- Sprinkle of confectioners' sugar
- ½ cup champagne brandy
- ½ cup Curaçao
- Mint leaves

Remove a lid off the most attractive of the melons. Take out all seeds and scoop out the melon in small pieces. Cut the second melon in half and dice in large pieces or scoop. Put all melon pieces in a bowl. Sprinkle with the confectioners' sugar, champagne brandy, and Curaçao. Stir and let sit for about an hour. To serve, put back in the melon shell, top with mint and cover with lid.

Crab Cakes with Sherry and Garlic Mayonnaise
Chicory Salad

Serves four

According to those scrutinizers of culinary origins, food historians, it's impossible to determine the individual, or the culture, to credit with being the first to eat crab. What historians can tell us about ancient crab eating is that the Greeks and Romans were universally unenthusiastic about it. And over the centuries various societies have viewed crabs unkindly: The word "crab"—in several languages—describes a person with a bad disposition. Cancer is not only the deadly disease, but the Latin word for crab. But surely much of the crab's bad rap is derived from its peculiar appearance: those scary looking claws, beady, antennaed eyes and its unpredictable and suspicious sideways walk. So whoever was that first crab-eater was likely both very hungry and very brave. Of course looks aren't everything, as anyone who likes seafood can attest. In the U.S. crab is second only to shrimp in shellfish popularity and our seventh most well-liked seafood.

My own experience with crab was limited by a childhood in the Midwest—handy for recognizing a good Wisconsin Limburger cheese, but not too helpful for encouraging an appreciation of ocean-run stuff, like fresh crab. Adulthood, and a move to the East Coast, brought the chance to catch up. My first taste was the gangly snow crab—just caught off Quebec's North Shore, it was sublimely poached in a wine court-bouillon by my French-Canadian hosts. Next I traveled to Alaska, and in the restaurant atop the Captain Cook Hotel, overlooking Cook Inlet in Anchorage, I ate Crab Imperial—lump crabmeat in a sherry white sauce—made with king crab. Several years later in Southeast Alaska, I helped the chef from the Glacier Country Inn bait jerry cans with fish heads to lure in the Dungeness crabs. He delicately steamed the huge crabs, served them with melted butter, his poppy seed bread, and kitchen-garden arugula salad. And then came my introduction to blue crabs—not steamed but as a cake—and true passion was born. True blue crab from the Chesapeake is now difficult sometimes to come by. But those in the business—my brother being one—assured me that imported Southeast Asia crab is very similar to the blue. And if my brother's pasteurized crab from Vietnam is any indication, I would say it's just as tasty and actually better cleaned than is our American blue. But this is a good recipe for all crab, regardless of nationality.

CRAB CAKES WITH SHERRY AND GARLIC MAYONNAISE

- 1 cup very finely minced celery
- 1 cup very finely minced onion
- 8-10 tbsp. unsalted butter
- 2 lbs. fresh crabmeat, cleaned of all cartilage
- 2 tbsp. Worcestershire sauce
- 1½ tsp. Tabasco sauce
- Juice of 1 lemon
- Salt and pepper
- 3 tbsp. very finely chopped parsley
- 4 cups fresh bread crumbs (see page 217)
- 3 egg yolks
- ¼ cup heavy cream
- 3 tsp. dry mustard
- 1 whole egg
- ¾ cup milk
- 2½ cups flour

Cook celery and onion in 4 tablespoons of the butter until translucent and wilted but not browned. Add this to the crabmeat along with the Worcestershire sauce, Tabasco sauce, lemon juice, salt and pepper, parsley, and 3 tablespoons breadcrumbs. Mix together the egg yolks, heavy cream and dry mustard and combine with the crabmeat. Refrigerate for 1 hour or until thoroughly cooled. Then gently shape into patties.

Beat the whole egg and milk together. Dip the patties into flour, then using a pastry brush, paint with egg/milk mixture and then dip into remaining bread crumbs. Do this gently, covering all surfaces. Place on a cooling rack and let rest in refrigerator for 30 minutes to 1 hour. To cook, heat 4 to 6 tablespoons of butter to sizzling and brown each crab cake about 4 minutes first side and 2½ to 3 on the second side. Serve with the sherry and garlic mayonnaise.

SHERRY AND GARLIC MAYONNAISE

⅓ cup sherry vinegar
8 garlic cloves, blanched, peeled and chopped finely
½ tsp. salt
2 tsp. prepared mustard
¼ tsp. ground pepper
Several dashes of cayenne
3 egg yolks
2 cups good olive oil

In a bowl combine: sherry vinegar, garlic, salt, mustard, pepper, cayenne. Let salt melt. Add egg yolks. Whisk until frothy and well combined. Add oil very slowly in a dribble until the mayonnaise seems to have started to thicken, then you may add the oil faster. When finished, taste for seasoning and adjust with salt, pepper, mustard, or sherry vinegar. Be sure to dissolve the salt in the sherry vinegar first as it will not dissolve as well in the mayonnaise. Whisk in a tablespoon of hot, hot water to finish it. This may be done in the food processor with no fuss/no mess.

CHICORY SALAD

    1 small head chicory
    1 head Boston lettuce
    1 small bunch watercress
    6 slices medium crisp bacon, or better yet, pancetta

For the dressing:
    3 tbsp. vinegar
    Salt and pepper
    1 tsp. prepared mustard
    1 tsp. tarragon, revived in a little hot water
    1 very small clove garlic, mashed and then chopped very fine
    ¼ cup olive oil

Wash the greens carefully. Shake dry and roll up in clean terry towels. (This can be done several hours before using, but keep in the towel in the fridge.) Combine all the ingredients for the dressing in a blender and blend on high. Toss salad with dressing. Add bacon or pancetta and then taste and adjust seasoning.

Szechwan Crab for Sunday Night Supper
White Rice with Soy Sauce on the Side
Stir Fried Pea Pods

Serves four

The white rice should be cooked the way you like it (I'm a fan of unconverted rice, and I especially like jasmine). Some very unusual and interesting soy sauces are now available in regular grocery stores and are worth experimenting with to find what you like.

The pea pods in this menu just need the tips cut and strings pulled off. Then sauté quickly in unsalted butter until hot. Season with salt and pepper.

SZECHWAN CRAB FOR SUNDAY NIGHT SUPPER

- 1¼ lbs. cooked, shelled crab cut into 2-inch pieces
- 6 scallions, chopped into ¹⁄₁₆-inch pieces, white part and ⅓ of the green
- 2 tbsp. ginger, peeled and chopped fine (1 inch of whole ginger = 1 tbsp. chopped ginger)
- 1 tbsp. Chinese rice wine
- 1 tsp. salt
- 4 eggs
- 5 tbsp. peanut oil
- ½ tsp. sugar

Mix together the crabmeat, scallions, all but ½ tablespoon of the ginger, the rice wine, and salt. Let sit for 20 minutes. Beat the eggs together and set aside.

Heat pan over medium high heat. Add oil. Drained the crabmeat/scallion mixture, reserving the liquid, and add it and the rest of the ginger and the sugar to the oil just as it is starting to bubble. Stir well for 1 to 2 minutes. Now add the wine liquid drained from the crabmeat mixture. Taste for seasoning. You may need up to ½ teaspoon of additional salt (don't worry if it seems like a lot). Fry another minute or so. Then add eggs, stirring constantly for another minute or two, until the eggs are thoroughly cooked. Serve immediately.

Freshwater Fish

I had a rather eclectic relationship with fish as a child. As a tiny little girl I have very far away memories of the commercial fishing boats on Lake Michigan, walking the beaches looking for the metal floats washed up from their nets, and my parents eating delicious "whitefish" for breakfast. But by the time I'd become old enough to catch the fish, the Great Lakes had become barren of edible fish and my greatest source and opportunity for catching and eating fish was gone. My parents resorted to eating fish that had been "brought in." The fish stores liked to claim that the fish had been flown in, but we could tell from the aroma and taste of the fish that it had actually travelled by wagon train and come down the Erie Canal. Fresh they were not. There were many years which passed where I stood firm on the belief that fish was not very tasty. In bits and pieces I began to learn something about fishing on my annual trips to Florida, but fishing and eating fish remained separate concepts for me for a long time.

The idea that the best fish to eat is the fish you've caught, and vice versa, came to me in two quick, hard lessons. As a ten-year-old cruising on a sailboat in the North Channel, I discovered something I'd never done before: fishing in the Great Lakes. Still rather barren of fish and me completely unknowledgeable about freshwater fishing, I was reduced to the little rock bass which lay along the pier where we were moored. The minnows netted proved excellent bait and I caught literally 50 or 60 little rock bass. Catch and release was not a concept I knew, and the little fish lay scattered on the dock. A passing gentleman, seeing the litter of dead fish exclaimed, "I hope you intend to eat every one of those." It was as if an enormous tidal wave of realization came over me: Most people eat what they catch! And as I looked at all those dead fish I understood what a dreadful thing I had done. Only the excuse of providing sustenance could have absolved me.

Clearly there was no brain in this pathetic fisherman but I was at least now armed with a new conscience (and primed for the concept of catch-and-release).

I did have the good sense to travel East and marry a fisherman. Although at this point I realized that morally it was tasteless to not eat what you caught and kept, I still was a little slow to understand the self-serving benefits of it all. Ed and I were invited up to Maine to use a friend's lovely old log cabin for fishing. We had the place to ourselves. The seven hour car ride had been long, especially the last hour on dirt roads. We felt particularly welcomed as we drove up to the house and saw the caretaker waiting for us with a little stringer of native brook trout. He had just finished building a fire and was breaking off sticks to skewer the fish as we were unloading the car. We sat by the water eating the roasted brook trout. I'd had brook trout in restaurants in the Midwest before; were these fish related? Impossible! As that wave of conscience had washed over me, so now did a new wave of eating delight. A freshly caught, wild fish, simply cooked; this surely was the ultimate taste treat. From there to catching the fish myself and eating it fresh, the lesson was forever locked in my mind, heart and taste buds.

I have never tasted a fresh fish that I didn't like. Much of this cookbook is concerned with cooking and eating very fresh fish and is written on the premise that a good, fresh fish need not require much preparation—only apply heat. The fresher the fish, the simpler the recipe for its preparation. Please don't let yourself get seduced for the sake of culinary art into cooking sauces and court bouillons and complicated recipes for a fresh fish. There's no need to overdo the cooking. Save all that for the rest of the menu or an old fish. Relax, and think of fresh fish as your chance to cook the simplest, but most delicious food there is.

I have in many of the menus here tried very hard to keep the fish recipes simple because that's what makes the fish taste best. Sometimes I have made the rest of the menu more complicated to keep your interest up in the meal, but on other occasions I've complemented the simplicity of the fish recipe with a simple menu: Pumpkinseed-Fish-On-A-Stick with Homemade Chocolate Chip Cookies. If only that had been my first meal of a fish I'd caught, it never would have taken me twenty-five years to love to fish and eat the fish I catch.

Stream Fish

I think God really wanted us to eat the fish we catch, but He realized there were a bunch of pigs and over-eaters in the crowd and so to help curb overconsumption He invented the sport fisherman: a creature who would find it appealing just to catch the fish and would figure out a whole lot of excuses why we all should put the fish back and not eat it. The fishermen have used guilt, as in the case of the striped bass (our chemical effluents have been killing the fry in the Chesapeake), and other reasons, too, to very effectively make us put much of it back.

When we go fishing in Alaska for rainbow trout, the guides are very proud of the fact that they may have had to kill only one trout, or maybe none at all, that summer. They are very protective of those trout and tell the fishermen that they aren't worth catching to eat anyway because they don't taste very good. A trout that doesn't taste good, is this possible? Oh, yes, it's because the rainbows feed on carcasses of the spawned-out, dead salmon. They must taste terrible feeding on that stuff. If this logic followed we'd have likely eliminated all fish consumption. Note the lovely aroma and appeal of your chum bucket some time; and doesn't that sea worm look scrumptious? Unlike the duck that feeds on wild rice or the antelope that grazes on sage-scented grasses, fish aren't in general known for their gourmet diets. It probably is a little difficult to honestly say that carcass-eating rainbows taste any worse than the ones that eat lemmings or salmon eggs or insects.

There is perhaps more correlation between where the fish lives and its flavor than to how diet affects its flavor. It does seem that the little brookies, the Dolly Vardens, grayling or rainbow trout that swim in the beautiful wild waters of Alaska, British Columbia, or Montana or Maine are better eating than hatchery trout.

Or is it simply that we like to catch the fish in those places? God did intend for us to eat the fish we catch.

Breakfast Trout Cornbread

Serves four

BREAKFAST TROUT

- 4 ½-inch slices of pancetta (Italian cured bacon)
- 4 12-oz. trout, cleaned, whole
- Salt and fresh ground pepper
- 1 cup flour
- ½ cup clarified butter
- 1 tbsp. plus 2 tsp. pancetta fat
- 20 cherry tomatoes
- Lemon wedges

Slice the pancetta into ½-inch strips and sauté on low heat until almost crisp. Set on paper towels to drain. Rinse trout, drain; sprinkle with salt and pepper. Dredge in flour; shake off excess. Fry in hot butter and 1 tablespoon pancetta fat 3 to 4 minutes per side. Set on warm plates when done and sauté cherry tomatoes in same pan, adding 2 teaspoons pancetta fat to the pan. Reheat the pancetta strips with the tomatoes. Divide among the plates and garnish with lemon wedges.

CORNBREAD

- 1½ cups cornmeal
- 2 tsp, baking powder
- 1 tsp. salt
- 2 tbsp. sugar
- ¼ cup flour
- 1 tbsp. finely diced sweet red pepper
- 3 tbsp. bacon drippings
- 2 eggs
- 1 cup buttermilk
- Butter for greasing the pan

Sift together the cornmeal, baking powder, salt, sugar and flour. Sauté the red pepper in the bacon fat. Beat the eggs, add the buttermilk and red pepper along with the bacon drippings. Now combine this with the dry ingredients. Butter either muffin tins or stick molds and bake in a 425° oven for 15 (molds) to 25 (tins) minutes.

Trout Fried
Stuffed Risotto Tomatoes
Zucchini
Strawberry Sponge

Serves four

TROUT FRIED

- 4 slices of French bread or a generous ½ cup of bread crumbs
- 2 tbsp. flour
- 2 trout, boned and filleted
- 1 egg
- 1 tsp. oil
- 1 tsp. water
- ¼ tsp. thyme
- 4 tbsp. unsalted butter
- Salt and pepper
- Lemon wedges

Process four slices of dry French bread in your food processor and sift through a wire mesh strainer. Put the flour on a plate and dust both sides of the fish. Combine the egg, oil, water and thyme and using a pastry brush, paint the fillets with this mixture. Now dip the trout into breadcrumbs and rest on a cake rack to dry. This can be done ½ hour before cooking. (If you leave the skin on put flour only on the skin side. Use the egg mixture and crumbs for the flesh side only.) Heat the butter in a large skillet until very hot. Put in fish and cook only a few minutes on each side. It will be very crispy on the outside and moist on the inside. The fish may be kept warm for a few minutes. Serve with lemon wedges.

STUFFED RISOTTO TOMATOES

For risotto:
- 4 oz. unsalted butter or a mixture of butter and olive oil
- 1 shallot, chopped very fine
- 1 cup Italian Arborio rice

    4-5 cups hot chicken stock
          Salt and pepper
          Pinch of saffron threads (optional)

In a heavy-bottomed, fry pan, heat butter. Sauté the shallot until translucent. Add rice. Cook, stirring until it becomes very white, shiny and very hot to touch. Then, over medium-high heat, add only enough hot stock so that the rice is just covered. Holding the handle of the pan, firmly swish the rice around and around. Do this every 2 to 3 minutes, keeping a low simmer going in the pot in between. This is so the rice won't stick. (If you weaken and stir the rice, then you must continue to stir until done.) As soon as you can distinguish the grains of rice again, then add another ½ cup of fluid. Keep swirling the pot and adding more fluid as it becomes absorbed. Taste when you feel it is nearly finished. It should be firm to the bite, with a tender, creamy texture—not too dry and not too runny. Season with salt and pepper. If using saffron, dissolve in the hot broth and add halfway through or with the very last addition of the broth. The nearer the end it is added, the stronger the taste.

    4 medium-sized tomatoes, ripe but firm
       Salt and pepper
       Dribble of oil
    2 tbsp. tomato purée
    2 tbsp. Parmesan cheese
       Sprinkle of bread crumbs
       Dots of butter

Remove tops and carefully scoop out seeds. Sprinkle with salt and pepper. Dot with oil and bake at 425° for 5 to 6 minutes. Remove from oven, drain juices and save. To the cooked risotto stir in the purée, Parmesan cheese, and the juices you reserved from the tomatoes. This can be done several hours ahead. Stuff each of the tomatoes with risotto and sprinkle with fresh bread crumbs. Dot with butter and bake at 425° for 10 to 15 minutes.

ZUCCHINI

  8 5 to 6-inch firm zucchini
2-3 tbsp. unsalted butter
  1 small clove garlic, chopped fine (optional)
      Salt and pepper

Cut both ends off the zucchinis. Cut in half lengthwise and then in half again so that each zucchini is in 4 long pieces. Cut each piece into ⅛-inch thick strips and then cut the strips in half. Melt butter. When very hot, add zucchini and garlic. Cook over medium high heat until soft. Season with salt and pepper and serve.

STRAWBERRY SPONGE

1 supermarket sponge cake
3 tbsp. framboise or Grand Marnier, or rum
4 egg yolks
⅓ cup sugar
¼ tsp. salt
1 cup heavy cream
1 tsp. vanilla extract
1 pint strawberries, washed, hulled and halved
    Several tbsp. melted currant jelly

Paint the sponge cake with a tablespoon or so of the framboise if you have it or Grand Marnier or even rum will do. Mix the egg yolks and sugar in a bowl with a whisk. Add salt and cream. Mix well but do not whisk to a foam. Transfer to a heavy bottomed sauce pan. Put over high or medium high heat and stir constantly with a wooden spoon (that means touching the bottom of the pan as you stir) until the custard begins to thicken and the surface of the custard becomes very smooth. Pour immediately through a strainer into another bowl and whisk to cool to stop the cooking. Then add two tablespoons of the liqueur and the vanilla and chill for several hours stirring occasionally. Spread the custard on the cake base and top with strawberries and glaze with the melted currant jelly. If not served at once, it may be chilled for a bit. Just bring it out of the refrigerator 15 minutes or so before eating.

Streamside Trout with Potatoes
Brownies

Serves four

For the best brownie recipe, see page 49.

STREAMSIDE TROUT WITH POTATOES

- 4 ½-inch thick slices of pancetta
- 4 medium potatoes, cleaned and chopped with skin on, cut into bite size pieces
- 4 stalks celery, cleaned and chopped
-   Salt and pepper
- 4 trout, cleaned and scaled

Slice the pancetta into ½-inch strips and sauté till almost crisp. (Pancetta is a cured Italian bacon. It is round in shape, at most deli counters, and may be eaten cooked, or uncooked. If you don't wish to carry it on your fishing trip, then cook it at home and bring the rendered grease.) Spoon out a little of the fat into a cup (to cook the fish in), add the potatoes and celery to the rest. Cover and cook till nicely browned, turning once or twice. Season with salt and pepper. Push aside and add the extra fat and fish. Cook the fish until the tails are just crispy and season with salt and pepper.

Poached Steelhead Trout with Lemon Butter Sauce
Fava Beans with Asparagus
Strawberries and Crème Anglaise

Serves four

Fresh fava beans are hard to find, especially anywhere outside of California, and usually obtainable only in the spring. But they are worth a hard search. Skip the canned version.

POACHED STEELHEAD TROUT WITH LEMON BUTTER SAUCE

- ½ cup plus 2 tbsp. vinegar
- 1½ qts. water
- 1 tbsp. salt
- 2 peppercorns, crushed
- Pinch thyme
- ½ bay leaf
- 1 onion, thinly sliced
- 1 carrot, sliced
- ¼ cup white wine
- Salt and pepper
- 2 shallots, chopped fine and sautéed in butter
- 8 oz. plus 1 tbsp. unsalted butter
- 4 steaks, ¾ to 1-inch thick. One steak per person should do, depending on the size of the fish.

Make a court bouillon by combining ½ cup vinegar, water, 1 tablespoon salt, peppercorns, thyme, bay leaf, onion and carrot and bringing to a boil. Cook 45 minutes. Strain and let cool.

Now combine together the 2 tablespoons of vinegar, wine, salt and pepper and cooked shallots and reduce by ½ to ⅔. Set aside.

Return the court bouillon to the stove and bring to a boil. Plunge the fish steaks into the bouillon and bring back to boil. Cover and remove from the heat. The steaks should take 7 to 8 minutes. Drain the fish and place on warm plates.

Return the vinegar wine reduction to heat and at a hot but not boiling temperature, add the 8 ounces of butter in small bits, whisking constantly. The sauce will become foamy and white. Serve immediately on the fish.

FAVA BEANS WITH ASPARAGUS

3-4 lbs. fava beans
1 lb. asparagus
2 tbsp. unsalted butter
Salt and pepper

Fava beans are a wonderful Spring vegetable. Big supermarkets will probably carry them as well as Italian markets. A lot of tedious work is involved in preparing them, but you may only eat them once a year, so it's worth it for the taste and the fact that they mean Spring is here. Remove fava beans from their pods. Peel the outer skin from each bean (it is worth it, I promise). Steam until just done—about 5 minutes. Refresh with ice water and drain. Remove the tips from the asparagus and use the stalks for soup another day. Blanch or steam the tips until just done. Refresh in ice water and drain. This can all be done in the morning. Cook the butter until sizzling (you could use ½ bacon fat if you wish). Add beans and asparagus. Cook until vegetables are heated through. Season with salt and pepper. Serve.

STRAWBERRIES WITH CRÈME ANGLAISE

- 4 egg yolks
- ¼ cup sugar
- Pinch of salt
- ½ cup milk
- ½ cup heavy cream
- 1 tbsp. liqueur (Grand Marnier is good) or vanilla
- 1 pt. fresh strawberries, cleaned and hulled

Whisk together the yolks, sugar, and salt. Combine the milk and cream and whisk that together with the yolk combination. Cook over a medium high heat stirring constantly until it thickens quite suddenly. Remove from the heat, strain and whisk cool. Add the liqueur or vanilla and spoon over the strawberries.

Trout with Noisette Butter
Sautéed Cucumbers
Dilled New Potatoes

Serves four

TROUT WITH NOISETTE BUTTER

4 trout
1 tbsp. olive oil, plus sprinkles for rubbing
Salt and pepper
Flour for dredging
8 tbsp. unsalted butter
Lemon juice

Clean the fish, removing intestines and gills. Wash and dry the fish and rub with oil and sprinkle with salt and pepper. Dredge in flour and shake off excess. Cook 4 tablespoons butter over medium heat until it is a very pale brown. Remove from heat and it will continue to cook a little more. If it appears to be turning color too fast, pour it into a cool pan to stop the cooking. Set this browned or noisette butter aside for the sauce. Heat remaining 4 tablespoons of butter and the tablespoon of oil together on medium-high until just about to sizzle. Add the trout and sauté until one side is golden and then turn and finish the other side. Remember, the second side will take a little less time. Serve the fish immediately, sprinkled first with lemon juice and then pour on the hot noisette butter.

SAUTÉED CUCUMBERS

4 cucumbers peeled, halved lengthwise, and seeded and cut into ¼-inch thick slices
2 tbsp. unsalted butter
Salt and pepper

Sauté in the hot butter until just tender. Season with salt and pepper.

DILLED NEW POTATOES

3 new potatoes per person
1 tbsp. chopped fresh dill
Salt and pepper

Boil or steam the new potatoes and then sprinkle with the dill, salt, and pepper.

Grilled Char with Tarragon and Shallot Butter
Pasta with Fresh Corn and Basil
Sautéed Cherry Tomatoes
The Best Brownies

Serves four

GRILLED CHAR WITH TARRAGON AND SHALLOT BUTTER

- 1½ sticks unsalted butter
- 1 tbsp. dried tarragon
- 3-4 shallots finely chopped
- Salt and pepper
- 1 dash Worcestershire sauce
- 4 char steaks
- Olive oil for basting

Make the compound butter in advance. Whip the butter until light and fluffy. Add tarragon, shallots, salt, pepper, and Worcestershire. Mix well and mound onto plastic wrap. Form into a cylinder and freeze for 24 hours. Bring to room temperature before using. Brush the char with oil and cook 6 to 8 minutes per side. Place pats of the compound butter on each steak and serve.

PASTA WITH FRESH CORN AND BASIL

- 1 lb. pasta
- 1 cup heavy cream, reduced by ½
- 1 tsp. dried basil, cooked with the cream
- 1½ cups cooked fresh corn
- Salt and pepper
- Pinch cayenne pepper
- Lots of fresh basil for garnish

While the pasta is cooking, reduce the cream with the dried basil. Add cooked corn. Season with salt and pepper and cayenne and combine with the cooked pasta, check for seasoning again and serve.

SAUTÉED CHERRY TOMATOES

- 24 cherry tomatoes
- 2 tbsp. unsalted butter
  Several sprigs of dill (or your choice; dried herbs work, too)
  Salt and pepper

Prick each cherry tomato with a pin to prevent the tomato skins from bursting and remove the green tops. Sauté in the butter till hot and sprinkle with chopped herbs and salt and pepper. Serve.

THE BEST BROWNIES

- 2 oz. unsweetened chocolate
- 1 stick unsalted butter
- 1 cup sugar
- 2 eggs
- 1 tsp. vanilla
- ¼ cup flour
- ¼ tsp. salt
- 1 cup chopped walnuts

Preheat oven to 325°. Melt together the chocolate and butter and then stir in the sugar. Beat together the eggs and vanilla and add them to the chocolate mixture. Now quickly stir in the flour, salt and chopped nuts. Spread in a greased 8 by 8-inch pan and bake 40 to 45 minutes at 325°. Do not overcook or they will be dry. Cake tester should just come out clean. Let cool in pan. Then cut in squares and remove. The first brownie will be hard to get out and may stick and crumble. Do not be deterred. These are the best brownies.

Pan Poached Grayling
Sautéed Potatoes with Chanterelles and Thyme
Green Salad
Fresh Fruit with Lightly-whipped Cream
Almond Cookies

Serves four

When I think of eating grayling, I always think of a streamside meal. This would be a good menu streamside especially if you did the chopping of herbs and whatnot before leaving home and had them ready to go in a baggie. Then lay the grayling fillets in foil, pour the wine over them and sprinkle the pre-chopped herbs, parsley, celery, and shallots from their baggie over the fish and seal the foil. Wrap again and cook in the coals of a wood fire. The potatoes and chanterelles can be done in a fry-pan over the coals, too. The fruit and cookies should be pre-prepared and ready to go. Just whip a little cream and you have a most elegant streamside dinner.

PAN POACHED GRAYLING

- 1 tsp. chopped parsley stems
- 1 small rib celery, peeled and diced
- 2 tsp. finely chopped shallots
- 3-4 tbsp. unsalted butter
- ⅔ cup white wine
- 4 fillets
- Salt and pepper
- (Optional—any chopped fresh herbs, such as tarragon, parsley, chives)

Sauté the parsley stems, celery, and shallots in 1 tablespoon butter. Add the wine and simmer for a few minutes. Add the fish. Cover and reduce heat and cook until just tender. Remove the fish and reduce the liquid by ½ over high heat. Lower the heat and whisk in the remaining butter. Season with salt and pepper. Stir in the herbs if you've chosen to use any. It is fine without. Pour over fish and serve.

SAUTÉED POTATOES WITH CHANTERELLES AND THYME

- 2 cups fresh chanterelle mushrooms, coarsely chopped
- 1 tbsp. bacon fat
- 5 tbsp. butter
- 4 medium potatoes, peeled, washed and dried and cut into medium chunks
- Salt and pepper
- ½ tsp. thyme

Rinse chanterelles and coarsely chop. Dry sauté the mushrooms until all water is evaporated from the mushrooms and remove from the pan. In the same pan melt bacon fat and 3 tablespoons of the butter until hot and sizzling. Add potatoes and sprinkle with salt and pepper. Cover and cook slowly. Let them brown slowly as they cook, stirring from time to time. At the same time, sauté the mushrooms in the remaining butter for 1 minute over medium high heat. Lower the heat and sprinkle with salt and pepper. Cook until all juice has evaporated stirring all the while. Add these to the cooked potatoes and sprinkle with thyme. Taste for seasoning and serve.

GREEN SALAD

- 1 tbsp. vinegar
- 1 tsp. prepared mustard
- ½ cup olive oil
- 1 tsp. basil
- Salt and pepper
- 1 head Boston, red, oak leaf, or Bibb lettuce (no strong tastes)

Blend all but the lettuce in the blender on high speed. Toss with the lettuce.

For the fresh fruit, whip 1 cup cream lightly with a little liqueur or rum and 1 teaspoon confectioners' sugar.

ALMOND COOKIES

  1 cup unsalted butter, softened
½ cup sugar
¼ tsp. salt
½ tbsp. grated orange rind
    Dash of almond extract
  2 cups flour
    Toasted slivered almonds

Cream the butter into the sugar and salt. Whip till fluffy. Add orange rind and almond extract and mix. Blend in the flour. Form the dough into two disks, wrap each in plastic wrap and refrigerate until it is firm, at least a half hour. Working with one disk at a time, remove from fridge, let soften on a lightly flour surface just enough to be workable. Cover disk with a large sheet of plastic wrap and roll out on a lightly floured surface and cut with a cookie cutter. If you have it, use a fish cookie cutter to flatter the fishermen. Place on a cookie sheet lined with parchment paper, sprinkle with toasted almond slivers and bake at 350° till just starting to brown around the edges (about 7 minutes or so). Remove cookies and let sit on the sheet for 5 minutes, then use a spatula to put cookies on a rack to cool.

Leftover Char Risotto
Your Nice Green Salad
Parmesan Rolls
Apricot Crème Brulée

Serves four

LEFTOVER CHAR RISOTTO

- 2 red peppers
- 1 green pepper
- 6 oz. unsalted butter or a mixture of butter and olive oil
- 2 onions, chopped very fine
- 1½ cups Italian Arborio rice
- 4-5 cups hot chicken stock
- 2 tbsp. chopped Italian parsley
- 1½ cups any leftover char, broken into pieces, fat and bones removed.

First, halve the peppers and take out the seeds (or use whole). Place them cut side down on a piece of foil in the broiler and broil them 2 to 3 minutes until the skins are black. Remove and let cool. Peel the black skin off, remove the seeds and slice the peppers into pieces.

Then, in a heavy-bottomed, wide saucepan, heat 4 ounces of the butter. Sauté onions until translucent. Add rice. Cook, stirring until it becomes very white, shiny and very hot to touch. Then, over medium-high heat, add only enough hot stock so that the rice is just covered. Holding the handle of the saucepan, firmly swish the rice around and around. Do this every 2 to 3 minutes, keeping a low simmer going in the pot in between. This is so the rice won't stick. (If you weaken and stir the rice, then you must continue to stir until done.) As soon as you can distinguish the grains of rice again, then add another ½ cup of fluid. Keep swirling the pot and adding more fluid as it becomes absorbed. Taste when you feel it is nearly finished. It should be firm to the bite, and tender, creamy texture—not too dry and not too runny. In the meantime, sauté the peppers separately (red from green) in a little butter and sprinkle parsley over them. Combine the risotto, peppers and char and check for seasoning.

PARMESAN ROLLS

- ⅔ cup warm milk
- 2 tsp. dry yeast
- 1 tsp. honey
- 2½ cups, plus 2 tbsp. for dusting, all-purpose flour
- 1¼ cups grated Parmesan
- ½ tsp. salt
- 3 eggs
- 5 tbsp. softened unsalted butter
- 1 tbsp. water

In a standing mixer fitted with a dough hook pour in half of the warm milk and add the yeast and honey. Let this stand until the yeast foams a bit—about 5 minutes. Whisk together in a separate bowl, the flour, Parmesan, and salt until well blended. Add this to the yeast/milk mixture along with the remaining ⅓ cup warm milk and blend on low. Increase the speed to medium and add 2 of the eggs, one at a time, making sure each is well blended and continue mixing until a soft dough forms, about 3 minutes. Beat in butter a tablespoon at a time and continue mixing for another couple minutes. Scrape the dough down—it'll be very sticky—so it forms a ball in the center of the bowl and then sprinkle with the 2 tablespoons of flour. Cover with a cloth and let rise until double, about 2 hours.

Turn dough out onto a floured surface and divide into 12 pieces. Form each piece into a ball, rolling it around on the floured surface, and then place in a buttered 9-inch layer cake tin. Each ball should be a ½-inch or so apart. Cover with cloth again and let rise until double and the rolls are touching each other, about an hour. Combine the last egg with the water to make a wash and brush the tops of the rolls with it. Place in a 375º oven for 20 to 25 minutes or until golden. Turn out onto a cooling rack, let cool for 20 minutes and serve. (The rolls once cooled also can be frozen.)

APRICOT CRÈME BRULÉE

I have determined after some experimentation that how long to cook this in the oven is, logically, somewhat dependent on how long you cook it on top of the stove. It's done atop the stove when the steam is rising off the egg mixture and is clearly thickening, especially at the bottom of the pan. If you've been patient and let the egg mixture thicken atop the stove, 30 minutes should be fine in the oven—at least for a soft custard.

- 8-10 dried apricots
- 1 cup apple juice
- 6 eggs
- 5 tbsp. sugar
- 3 cups heavy cream (or 1½ cups heavy cream and 1½ cups whipping cream)
- 1 tbsp. vanilla
- ½-⅔ cup dark brown sugar

In a small heavy-bottomed saucepan cover apricots with just enough apple juice to cover the tops; use good apple juice. Bring to a low simmer and cook with a lid until the apricots become very soft and mushy. Let cool and purée in a food processor. Spread apricot purée on bottom of a round, stoneware baking dish that is about 11 inches or so in diameter.

Make the custard by separating the eggs, then beat the yolks and combine well with the white sugar and cream. Heat the mixture over a medium heat stirring constantly with a whisk until you can see steam beginning to rise and the custard is starting to form around the edge of the pot. Remove from the burner and add the vanilla. Pour through a strainer into the baking dish with the purée in the bottom. Put the dish on a cookie sheet that has sides and surround it with an inch or so of boiling water. Bake it in a preheated oven at 300° for 30 minutes or so, until the custard is just setting around the edges but is still soft in the middle. Remove from the oven and let it sit in the water-bath while it cools—about 30 minutes. Then refrigerate the custard for at least two hours or overnight. Just before serving sprinkle the custard with the brown sugar and put the dish back on the cookie sheet and this time surround it with ice cubes. Put it under a very hot broiler for a minute or two until the brown sugar burns a bit and forms a nice hard crust. Serve immediately or chill again and serve.

Steamed Whitefish
Squash, Broccoli, and Turnips in Wine
Orange Oranges

Serves four

STEAMED WHITEFISH

- 1 handful white peppercorns
- 1 cup raspberry vinegar
- 3-4 lbs. whitefish fillets

Simmer the peppercorns together with the vinegar for about 10 to 15 minutes. Place a steamer rack over the vinegar and lay the fillets on top. Simmer for about 15 minutes.

SQUASH, BROCCOLI, AND TURNIPS IN WINE

- 3-4 white turnips, peeled and cut into slices ½-inch thick
- 2 yellow squash, sliced in ½-inch round slices
- ⅔ cup wine (white or red)
  A few basil leaves for the wine and fresh chopped basil for the squash
- 1 head broccoli, cut into florets
- 1 cup water

A pinch of thyme and a few crushed fennel seeds

In a tiered steamer, with the turnips on the bottom and squash on the top (the squash takes the least time to cook) combine the wine and basil leaves and steam for about 20 minutes. Just before done add the remaining chopped basil to the squash. Steam the broccoli over the water with the thyme and fennel seeds added to it until the broccoli is just tender, about 10 minutes. Arrange the three steamed veggies on a platter or plates. Season with salt and pepper or you may want to use soy sauce instead of salt for more flavor.

ORANGE ORANGES

    4 navel oranges
    3 tbsp., plus enough to sprinkle, Grand Marnier
    2 cups sugar
    1 cup water
    1 tsp. lemon juice

    With a vegetable peeler remove the orange part only of the skin from 2 of the oranges. Julienne into matchstick size pieces. Blanch in boiling water for 5 to 7 minutes and then rinse in cold water. Dry the orange rind with paper towels and let sit in the Grand Marnier. With a large sharp knife cut off both ends of all four oranges. Both ends means the rind and the white pith exposing the flesh. Stand them on end and remove all the peel and pith leaving 4 naked oranges. Then slice into ½-inch slices and arrange on a platter slightly overlapping or on individual plates. Sprinkle with additional Grand Marnier.

    Slowly bring to a boil sugar, water and lemon juice. Cook until 245°, at the hard ball stage. Stir a few tablespoons into the orange peel and Grand Marnier. With the remaining syrup, one spoon at a time, glaze the orange slices. Chill this for several hours and serve with the sugared rinds which you have drained.

Walleye and Pike

It has been said that necessity is the mother of invention. It is also the mother of some terrific meals.

We were visiting our friends, Dave and Kim Egdorf, who run a fish camp in the Bristol Bay region of Alaska. Dave and Ed were flying the last two guests in to Dillingham and picking up supplies. Kim and I had the luxury of lolling about camp for the few hours they were gone. We talked a lot about cooking, what it was like to cook every day for a camp full of fishermen, what problems were unique to cooking in the bush, what were some of her fish recipes. The talk was fun, but the two hours the men were supposed to be gone were stretching into three. Kim had wanted to get dinner cooking but needed the supplies to do so. The in-the-bush game of trying to hear the airplane's motor first was beginning to grow old with mirages of noises building, then destroying expectations. At long last the engine of Dave's Beaver could truly be heard; it was quite late but the daylight hours were still long in Alaska. The tardiness excuses were made and we waited for the supplies to be brought in. Gas cans and motor oil appeared, but where were the groceries? There was then a very quiet "discussion" between Dave and Kim.

"I gave you a grocery list!"

"No you did not!"

It, of course, didn't really matter who was supposed to give what to whom or who had lost what, the deed was done. (I am happy to report to all the wives reading this that the next day when I was fishing with Dave he was searching in his pockets for a twist-on lead weight and found the slip of paper—the list—he had so heartily denied having the night before.) We were now faced with nothing to eat for dinner and the nearest restaurant or grocery store many hundreds of miles away—by plane only.

Ah, but we had a river full of fish lying before us. Ed and Dave quickly grabbed rods and soon we were obliged with a wonderful pike. Kim made Pike Puffs, her own great tempura-like concoction that quickly became nearly my favorite fish recipe that she does. Dinner was spectacular.

Rarely am I truly hundreds of miles away from the nearest grocery store. But there are times with the New England weather or because of my own attitude the grocery store might as well be a hundred miles away. I get the greatest pleasure out of figuring out what I can make from what's left in the pantry. It's a game of letting the imagination run wild, with certain restraints. It also is a game which has forced the creation of many a great recipe, and is terrific mental and culinary exercise for when the fisherman returns home not with the anticipated salmon, but with pike. Don't run for this cookbook, improvise!

Pike Couscous
Cool Vegetables with Herb Mayonnaise
Grilled Pineapple

Serve four

Some people don't know about couscous. It is a grain, similar to grits or rice, which comes from North Africa. It is a nice alternative to the big three starches and is delicious.

PIKE COUSCOUS

- 2 cups chicken broth
- 10 tbsp. unsalted butter
- ¼ tsp. cumin
- ¼ tsp. coriander, ground
- Salt and pepper
- 2 cups couscous
- 2 pounds pike fillets, skinned and cut into 2-inch pieces
- 2 scallions, green part only, chopped
- Parsley, chopped finely
- 1 tsp. lemon rind, grated

In a saucepan, bring the chicken broth to a boil adding 6 tablespoons butter, the ground cumin and coriander; add salt and pepper. Stir in the couscous, cover pan and remove from the heat and let stand for 5 minutes. In a fry pan sauté the fish and scallions in 3 to 4 tablespoons butter over medium-high heat until the fish is done, 4 minutes or so. Season with salt and pepper. Add the hot fish and scallions, parsley and lemon rind to the couscous. Toss well with a fork, fluffing up the couscous at the same time to break up any lumps. Taste for seasoning, adding more salt and pepper if necessary and serve in large soup plates.

COOL VEGETABLES WITH HERB MAYONNAISE

As a first course, blanch a large variety of vegetables (broccoli, green beans, squash, carrots and cauliflower) and serve with a spiced or herb mayonnaise (see page 217 for mayonnaise). This can be arranged on individual plates or presented as a centerpiece to be eaten with each person having their own bowls of mayonnaise.

GRILLED PINEAPPLE

- 1 medium size ripe pineapple
- 1 tbsp. brown sugar
- 2 tbsp. Grand Marnier or Cointreau

Cut off the top, bottom and the sides of the pineapple with a large sharp knife. Remove the core and slice in thin slices, ½-inch thick or less. Grill until they start to brown. Sprinkle with the brown sugar and liqueur at the last minute and serve.

Sautéed Walleye with Noisette Butter and Shallots
Couscous
Broiled Tomatoes
Blancmange

Serves four

Broiled tomatoes are just that, slice them and run them under the broiler for a few minutes and season.

SAUTÉED WALLEYE WITH NOISETTE BUTTER AND SHALLOTS

- 8 shallots, peeled and sliced thin
- 2-3 tbsp. unsalted butter
- 2 lbs. walleye fillets, dusted with flour
- Salt and pepper

Cook the shallots in 1 tablespoon unsalted butter until they just start to turn a golden color and set aside. Sauté the fish in the remaining butter and top with shallots and the noisette butter. (You will need 1 stick unsalted butter, cooked until noisette, or browned. See page 191) Season with salt and pepper.

COUSCOUS

- 1 cup chicken stock
- 6-8 tbsp. unsalted butter, softened
- Salt and pepper and a pinch cayenne
- 1 cup couscous
- Chopped parsley

In saucepan bring stock to a boil and add 4 tablespoons butter, salt and pepper and cayenne. When melted, stir in couscous and cover pan and let stand 5 minutes. Add 2 or 3 more tablespoons soft butter and let stand another minute covered. Then fluff the couscous with a fork and season well with salt and pepper and chopped parsley.

BLANCMANGE

- 1 envelope gelatin with 1 tbsp. water
- 1 cup whole milk
- 3 cups heavy cream
- ⅔ cup sugar
- ¼ tsp. salt
- 3 tbsp. green chartreuse liqueur

Combine the gelatin and the water in a small custard cup. Set in a small frypan filled with hot water on low heat. This way the gelatin will melt without lumps. Combine milk and cream in a heavy bottom saucepan and scald. Remove from the heat and add the sugar, salt and stir to dissolve. Add the dissolved gelatin scraping the little custard cup well. Mix thoroughly by stirring and add 3 tablespoons green chartreuse. Pour blancmange into individual serving dishes and chill overnight.

Walleye en Papillotte
Pasta with Parmesan and Romano Cheeses
Green Salad with Oil and Vinegar
Honeydew Ice

Serves four

To use fresh grated cheeses in the pasta recipe is quite essential. Fresh pasta is also a nice touch, but it is possible to buy fresh pasta in the grocery store now. So unless the queen is coming to dinner or you've got a small child crazy to crank the pasta machine, buy this ready-made.

WALLEYE EN PAPILLOTTE

- 1 onion, sliced very thinly
- 3 shallots chopped finely
- 4 tbsp. unsalted butter and some for buttering the parchment
- Salt and pepper
- ⅔ cup white wine
- Rind of ½ an orange, with as little of the pith as possible, julienned and blanched
- 2 lbs. fillets
- Parchment paper
- 4 sprigs tarragon

Sauté the onions and shallots in the butter until translucent and starting to brown. Season with salt and pepper and add wine. Reduce the mixture until it becomes syrupy. Add orange rind (12 pieces) and remove from heat. Cut 4 pieces of parchment paper into hearts, 12 inches long and 10 inches wide at the top (the widest part) and lightly butter. Divide fish onto the 4 pieces of parchment, setting the fish onto the right side of the heart. Divide up the onion, shallots, orange rind on top and top this with a nice size sprig of tarragon. Fold up heart. Bring the left side over to the right side and seal the edges with many little narrow folds to keep the heart closed. When you get to the tip, twist it tight and tuck it in. Bake on a baking sheet in a preheated 400° oven for 10 to 15 minutes. Put directly on plates and open each heart at the table. The aroma with the tarragon and orange rind will be delicious.

PASTA WITH PARMESAN AND ROMANO CHEESES

    1 lb. fresh fettuccini pasta
       Salt and large cracked black pepper
    6 tbsp. unsalted butter at room temperature
    ½ cup fresh grated Parmesan cheese
    ½ cup fresh grated Romano cheese

Cook pasta according to directions and drain. Toss with salt and pepper and butter, then cheeses. Serve at once.

Have a green salad of Boston and Bibb lettuces with just oil, balsamic vinegar and salt and pepper.

HONEYDEW ICE

    1-2 honeydew melons (you want about 3-4 lbs. of flesh)
    3 tbsp. Midori liqueur or melon flavored liqueur
    6-8 tbsp. confectioners' sugar
       Juice from 2 lemons
       A pinch of salt
       Mint leaves for garnish

Open the melon, discard the seeds, and purée the flesh in a food processor or blender. Add to the purée the Midori, confectioner's sugar, lemon juice, and salt, tasting as you go to make sure the flavor is to your liking. Stir well, chill, taste again for flavor and balance. Make according to your ice cream machine's directions.

Pack the melon sorbet into parfait glasses and chill thoroughly. Garnish with mint sprigs or a strawberry cut and fanned out.

Walleye Steaks with Béarnaise Sauce
Cabbage Patch Pasta Salad
Apple Tart

Serves four

For the Apple Tart, see page 135

WALLEYE STEAKS WITH BÉARNAISE SAUCE

- 2 onions, chopped fine
- 1 carrot, chopped fine
- 3 shallots, chopped fine
- 3 tbsp. unsalted butter
- 1 bottle dry red wine
- ½ cup vinegar
- 6 cups water
- 1 tbsp. salt
- 10 white peppercorns
- 1 bay leaf
- 1 tsp. dried thyme
- 12-16 parsley stems
- 4 steaks, 1½ inches thick

Sauté the onions, carrot, and shallots in butter. Combine with the wine, vinegar, water, salt and peppercorns, bay leaf, thyme, and parsley stems and cook at a simmer for 30 minutes. Let cool. Now to cook the fish, bring this court bouillon to a rolling boil. Arrange the fish steaks on a rack placed into the court bouillon and bring back to a boil; cover and remove pan from heat. Let sit 8 to 10 minutes, check for doneness. When done, drain, season with salt and pepper and serve with béarnaise sauce.

BÉARNAISE SAUCE

¼ cup good wine vinegar
½ cup white wine
1 tbsp. dried tarragon, revived in a little hot water
1 tbsp. chopped parsley
3 medium shallots, chopped fine
  Salt and fresh cracked or ground pepper
3 egg yolks
½ lb. unsalted butter, melted

1 tsp. fresh tarragon, chopped
  Parsley sprinkles

Bring the vinegar, wine, revived dried tarragon, parsley, shallots, salt and pepper to a boil. Reduce heat and on a low simmer, cook until reduced by ⅔ (this may be done ahead and refrigerated). Lower heat to the lowest and add yolks, one by one, whisking very fast. Remove from heat, add warm, melted butter very slowly and continue to whisk. Strain through coarse strainer into bowl and add fresh chopped tarragon and parsley. Taste for seasoning; if you need to add more salt, mix it first with boiling water to dissolve before adding.

CABBAGE PATCH PASTA SALAD

- ½ lb. cooked pasta
- 2 tbsp. toasted sesame oil
- 1 cup julienned Savoy cabbage
- ¼ cup olive oil and some more for sautéing veggies
- 2 red peppers, julienned
- 2 yellow peppers, julienned
- 2 cups snow peas, de-strung and cut in half on the diagonal
- 2 tbsp. vinegar
- 1 tsp. prepared mustard
- Pepper
- 1 tsp. soy sauce
- 1 tbsp. fresh coriander

After you've cooked the pasta, toss it with the sesame oil. Sauté the cabbage very briefly in a little of the olive oil. Sauté red and yellow peppers separately in oil until cooked, but still retain some crunch. Blanch, drain and dry the snow peas. Now make a dressing by zipping in the blender for a few seconds the vinegar, mustard, pepper, soy sauce and chopped fresh coriander and ¼ cup oil. Toss all ingredients together with the dressing and taste for seasoning.

Lemon-Lime Walleye
Wild Mushroom and Potato Flan
Salad
Drunk Melons

Serves four

The recipe for the Drunk Melons can be found on page 145. The recipe for the green salad can be found in your head or by perusing the "Basics" chapter in this book for a good vinaigrette that will go over fresh lettuce.

LEMON-LIME WALLEYE

1½ sticks unsalted butter
   Grated rind of 2 limes, green part only
   Grated rind of 1 large lemon, yellow part only
1 garlic clove, very finely chopped
2 tsp. finely chopped parsley
   Salt and pepper
2 lbs. walleye fillets

Whip butter till soft and fluffy. Add the rest of the ingredients, except the fillets. Season to taste. Mix well. Mound on to plastic wrap. Form into a cylinder. Freeze 24 hours and bring to room temperature before serving. Grill or broil the walleye, adding some of the compound butter just before finished cooking and then slather with more after cooking. Serve at once.

WILD MUSHROOM AND POTATO FLAN

- 8 oz. fresh wild mushrooms cleaned, coarsely chopped (oyster mushrooms are good for this and readily available at many grocery stores)
- 2 tbsp. butter plus some for buttering the pan
- ⅔ cup cooked potatoes, coarsely chopped
- Salt and pepper
- Pinch of thyme for the potatoes
- 1½ cups milk
- ½ cup cream
- 3 whole eggs
- 2 egg yolks
- Watercress for garnish

Preheat the oven to 325°. Sauté the mushrooms in 2 tablespoons of butter. Season the cooked potatoes with salt, pepper, and a pinch of thyme. Have a kettle of boiling water ready. This recipe may be made in a 4-cup ring mold or in individual ½ cup capacity custard cups (use 8). Whichever is used, butter heavily with unsalted butter and set into a cake or roasting pan. Scald milk and cream. Cool a bit and slowly add the whole eggs and yolks stirring constantly. Season well with salt and pepper and strain into a pitcher. Pour a bit into each mold. Divide the mushrooms and potatoes into each mold and add the rest of the custard. Pour the boiling water into the roasting pan around the edges so the mold(s) will have water coming ⅔ up the sides. Cover the large pan lightly with tinfoil and cook 15 to 20 minutes. A custard is a custard. Do not overcook. It will continue cooking after being removed from the heat. A knife inserted half way down should just barely be clean. Let sit 5 minutes in the mold(s) and unmold by running a knife around the edge. Garnish around the edge with sautéed watercress.

Shad, Catfish, and Smelt

Shad and smelt are quite pretty little fish and when the run is on, fishing for them is truly an event. Clear, but long-ago, memories of fishermen at night ringing the concrete shores of Lake Michigan in downtown Chicago complete with torches and constant activity testify to the spectacle of smelt fishing. Catfish are certainly as tasty as shad or smelt, but certainly are not as pretty. Catfish are really ugly and the saying that the bravest man in history is the first man to have eaten a lobster probably holds true for the first man to have eaten catfish too; either that or he was very hungry.

As the catfish will testify, the outside look has nothing to do with the inside flavor. Really only in the case of an unknown species (as with the fish on the bridge) or with an obviously sick fish should ugliness be a deterrent to eating. This business of picking the parasites off the fish in order to get to the meat, although a closet practice, is something that is definitely disgusting. Yes, we know that the cooking will probably kill anything harmful, that restaurants are known to remove the parasites from the fish and serve the fish anyway to the customer who is none the wiser, and that the parasites will not harm the meat once removed. But why do this? It's revolting and takes away the appetite. Even if we get someone else to remove the little bugger while we retire from the kitchen, we still know it was there, don't we? There are more fish in the sea, feel no guilt at sending it off to the chum bucket or tossing it out. We all take enough risk as it is eating commercially prepared foods. Why risk the good name of freshly caught, personally cared for, and healthy fish for the sake of one not too healthy fish? It surely is better to save a strong stomach for skinning a catfish than de-bugging a salmon.

Fried Smelts with Noisette Butter
Fried Parsley
Grilled Pineapple with Strawberries

Serves four

FRIED SMELTS

- 3 eggs
- 2 tsp. corn oil, plus enough for deep-fat frying the fish
- 2 tsp. water
- Salt and pepper
- 2½ cups bread crumbs
- 2 tsp. thyme
- 16-20 smelts (depending on size and appetite), cleaned with the heads off. There is no need to bone them as the bones are easily removed at the table.
- 1 cup flour

In Imperial Rome smelts—or a small fish very much like smelt—were cooked in a custard. I believe they are better fried. Combine the eggs, 2 teaspoons of corn oil, water and salt and pepper and set aside. Now make the bread crumbs by taking French bread cut into slices and drying them in the oven at 300°. Then reduce to crumbs in a food processor or blender. Strain for uniformity of size and mix with the thyme. Rinse and dry smelts. Dredge in flour and shake off excess. Paint with egg mixture and roll in bread crumbs. Let rest on a cake cooling rack while the rest of the meal is prepared. They may be deep fried for about 1 minute (until golden) with the oil at 375° or you may fry them in an electric frying pan at 400°. In either case, after cooking drain on paper towels. They may be kept warm in the oven on racks.

NOISETTE BUTTER

2 sticks unsalted butter
1 tbsp. lemon juice

Cook the unsalted butter in a heavy bottomed saucepan constantly stirring until light brown. Remove from heat and let it continue to brown a bit more. (If it is browning too fast, pour the butter into another pan.) Stir in the lemon juice.

FRIED PARSLEY

1 large bunch parsley, washed and dried very well
¼ cup corn oil
Sea salt flakes

Deep fry the parsley in some corn oil in a heavy saucepan or sauté in some clarified butter until just crisp. Drain well on paper towels and sprinkle with salt just as you serve it.

GRILLED PINEAPPLE WITH STRAWBERRIES

1 medium-sized ripe pineapple
1 pint strawberries
1 tbsp. confectioners' sugar
2 tbsp. Grand Marnier or Cointreau
Mint leaves

Cut off the top, bottom and the sides of the pineapple with a large sharp knife. Remove the core and slice in thin slices about ½-inch thick or less. Grill until they start to brown and caramelize. Hull the strawberries and slice in half if large. Sprinkle with confectioners' sugar and Grand Marnier or Cointreau, toss and let sit several hours. To serve, place 4 slices of pineapple slightly overlapping on a plate and fill the center holes with the strawberries. Garnish with fresh mint if you can and be sure to provide fruit knives as well as forks, for the pineapple will be somewhat chewy.

The Best Catfish
Simple Green Salad
French Bread

Serves four

For a salad, you can invent one yourself, or refer to the "Basics" chapter at the back of this book for an interesting vinaigrette. Use it on the most healthy looking greens you can find in the grocery store. French bread, of course, can be purchased successfully everywhere. But as anyone who has spent a little time in France knows, the fresher the better. It is easy to make yourself. Just use a white bread recipe and a French bread pan. Be sure to brush the crust several times in the cooking with cold water so a hard crust will form.

THE BEST CATFISH

- ⅔ cup all-purpose flour
- ½ tsp. dried thyme
- ¼ tsp. salt
- A pinch of dried sage, plus 1 tsp.
- ⅛ tsp. cayenne pepper
- 4 grinds fresh black pepper
- 2 lbs. catfish fillets, cut into strips 1½ inches long and ½ inch or so wide
- 1 medium size eggplant, peeled and cut into 1½ by ½-inch pieces, salted and left to drain in a colander 10 minutes
- 5 tbsp. unsalted butter
- 5 tbsp. corn oil
- 2 boiling potatoes, peeled and cut into 1½ by ½-inch pieces (keep in cold water)
- 2 garlic cloves, chopped fine
- 1 tsp. grated lemon rind
- Salt and pepper

Combine the flour with the thyme, salt, a pinch of sage, and both peppers. Dredge fish well in seasoned flour and shake off all excess. Let rest on cake cooling racks until ready to cook. The eggplant should now be rinsed, drained, dried and tossed in the flour. In a heavy-bottomed skillet (2 pans at once is easiest), start with 1 tablespoon butter and 1 tablespoon of oil and continue to add as needed. Heat until sizzling and add catfish (not to be crowded) and sauté until browned. Set aside on warmed platter. Sauté eggplant and potatoes in separate pans until golden. Add together. Melt any remaining butter or use more, in empty pan and add the garlic. Sauté for 1 minute, then add 1 teaspoon dried sage and the catfish, eggplant and potatoes. Grate lemon peel over it all. Toss well and season to taste with salt and pepper.

Fried Catfish
Cole Slaw
Grits
Broiled Persimmons

Serves four

There is nothing so basic as catfish, or grits, or cole slaw. They are as basic as a hamburger, and just as easy to get too casual about and wreck. Of course, attention should be paid to the recipes for the best results, it's worth it as these dishes are delicious.

FRIED CATFISH

- 2 eggs
- 2 tsp. milk
- 2 tsp. oil
- 2 tsp. salt
- ½ tsp. fresh ground pepper
- 2 lbs. catfish fillets, pat dry
- Flour for dusting
- 2 cups cornmeal, yellow or white
- Bacon fat
- Corn oil

Mix eggs, milk, oil, salt and pepper. Season fish very lightly with salt and pepper. Dust fish with flour. Paint with egg mixture and roll in cornmeal. Let rest on cake cooling racks until ready to cook. In heavy skillet, melt a combination of bacon fat and corn oil to ⅛-inch deep. When the oil is hot, fry fish until brown on one side and repeat for other side, but not quite as long.

COLE SLAW

Deli-bought, your mom's recipe, or see page 88.

GRITS

- 3 cups boiling water with 1½ chicken bouillon cubes added to it. (Knorr is a good brand)
- 4 tbsp. unsalted butter, sliced
- ⅛ tsp. cayenne and a few grinds Fresh pepper
- ¾ cup grits (not instant)
- 2 eggs
- ½ lb. grated gruyere or sharp cheddar

Bring water and bouillon cubes to a boil and add butter, cayenne and fresh pepper. Then add grits. Cook, stirring over medium heat until the mixture thickens and becomes the consistency of oatmeal. Remove from heat and let cool slightly. Add eggs one at a time, stirring quickly to incorporate each one and then add cheese. Mix well and check for seasoning. Cook in a 350° preheated oven for 1 hour.

BROILED PERSIMMONS

- 4 persimmons, not too ripe
- 4 tbsp. unsalted butter
- 2 tsp. sugar
- Sherry

Cut persimmons in half. Broil till warm. Remove seeds and top each half with butter and sugar. Return to broiler and cook till butter is melted. Sprinkle with sherry and serve.

Sorrel Soup
Shad Roe
Pink New Boiled Potatoes
Rhubarb Fool

Serves four

SORREL SOUP

6 shallots, finely chopped
6 tbsp. unsalted butter
4 cups sorrel, clean and coarsely chopped
4 cups hot chicken stock
½ tsp. salt
Fresh ground pepper
4 tbsp. flour
2 cups heavy cream
Salt and pepper
A squeeze of lemon juice

Sorrel is one of the first things up in the garden. Sauté shallots in 2 tablespoons of the butter until soft and transparent. Add sorrel. Stir once or twice. Lower heat and cover and cook until the sorrel has completely wilted. Add chicken stock and salt and pepper. Simmer gently about 15 minutes. Blend in processor. Melt the remaining 4 tablespoons of butter. When sizzling add the flour. Cook on medium heat for 4 minutes, stirring constantly. Take off the heat and add the hot stock mixture. Pour in about a cup, whisk to mix then add the rest, stirring. Bring back to a simmer. Remove from heat and add heavy cream and chill. Before serving, adjust to taste with salt and pepper and lemon juice.

SHAD ROE

4 sets of roe
Flour for dredging
Salt and pepper
4 tbsp. unsalted butter
Lemon wedges

Wash 4 sets of roe. Do not separate the sets unless they are already separated and if the roe are large you will need less. Remove clots, etc. Gently parboil for about 4 minutes to toughen the outer membrane a little so it is less apt to burst. Let cool and then roll in flour seasoned with salt and pepper. Sauté 4 to 5 minutes per side in the butter. Serve with lemon wedges.

SHAD

If you are going to eat the shad, serve it with a white butter sauce. Try to get someone else to bone it, as it is very difficult. Salt and pepper each side of the fish. Spread with soft butter and squeeze the fish back together and broil it 6 minutes per side.

PINK NEW BOILED POTATOES

1 stick unsalted, softened butter
Salt and pepper
1 tsp. chopped chives
3 new potatoes per person

Combine the softened butter with the salt, pepper, and chives. Boil the potatoes for about 20 minutes or until soft. Drain and crack open. Spread with the butter mixture.

RHUBARB FOOL

- 3 lbs. young rhubarb
- 1 cup sugar
- Zest of 1 lemon
- 1½ tsp. vanilla extract
- 2 cups heavy cream
- 2 tsp. confectioners' sugar
- ¼ tsp. ground cloves

Peel the rhubarb using a sharp knife. There is an almost transparent outside skin which comes off very easily. Then slice into very thin slices. This is most easily done when the rhubarb is held bunched together. In a heavy saucepan with a lid, put the rhubarb and the sugar and cover tightly and cook over low heat for 10-15 minutes. Remove the lid and raise heat and cook until excess liquid has evaporated, stirring constantly. It will become thick like applesauce. Be sure to stir it or the rhubarb will scorch. When ready, remove from the heat and add lemon zest and vanilla and set aside to cool. Whip the cream with the confectioners' sugar and the ground cloves until stiff. Fold the rhubarb in gently and chill.

Bass and Panfish

I sure have tried a lot of methods for preserving fish. I've tried freezing the fish whole, I've tried freezing the fish cleaned, I've tried freezing just the fillets or steaks. I've tried smoked fish and I've tried dried and salted fish, I've even tried canning fish. Ted was kind enough to make a presentation to me one time of some beautiful yellow perch which he'd handily frozen whole in a wax milk carton filled with water. The perch were delicious, but I fear his preservation receptacle may become a rare and difficult commodity to find with the transition to plastic milk cartons.

One time when we were fishing for Atlantic salmon in northern Quebec we hit a blitz of migrating fish and caught more than anticipated—certainly more than we could eat before the bush plane came to get us that evening. So we decided to try and haul the fish out with us and commandeered several Styrofoam fishing boxes we'd luckily found in an abandoned fishing camp. We packed the boxes chock-o-block full of fish and glacier ice and waited for the bush pilot to show up, which took quite a bit longer than we anticipated since he'd forgotten us—entirely. (Ah, the vagaries caused by alcohol!) He did eventually remember us and appeared, but two days late and that caused us to miss the weekly southbound train. Not to worry, there was a plane, but even glacial ice doesn't last forever in a Styrofoam box. There was quite a bit of slush oozing out of the boxes onto the baggage carousel of Air Canada when we arrived in Boston and the condition of the fish was, well, we wondered about it. Miraculously the fish, which were then refrozen, provided us with many wonderful, memorable meals. I never quite understood it given what the poor fish had been through to get to our table.

Some fish do, I believe, translate better to freezing or smoking or salting or canning than do others. Certainly salmon seems more stable and resilient than other fish, as is evidenced by the Air Canada salmon. And if you've never tasted a certain species of fish fresh before, what have you to compare it to when you eat it smoked or salted for the first time? This was true of the yellow perch Ted gave us. Indeed they were good, but I didn't know till some time later how good they could really be.

The relative merits of all the various preservation techniques are difficult to assess. The reality is that every method imposes changes to the fiber and flavor of the meat and is different than the fresh flavor. Smoked fish does not taste like fresh fish. This is not to say that smoked fish is bad, it is simply different.

One thing is for certain, the species of fish in this chapter are my five top candidates to avoid freezing, smoking, salting, or canning. These fish are plentiful, relatively easy to catch, well distributed geographically, and should only be eaten fresh.

Chicken Consommé
Almond Butter Smallmouth Bass
Sautéed Tomatoes
Fried Bread
The Pretty Easy Dessert

Serves four

CHICKEN CONSOMMÉ

- 1 small onion, thinly sliced
- 3 carrots, peeled and chopped small
- 1 stack celery, chopped small
- 1 tbsp. unsalted butter
- 8 cups clear chicken broth (If you do not have homemade, use the least salty boxed or canned you can find.)
- 1 bunch watercress, just the leaves

Sauté the onion, carrots, and celery in the unsalted butter over medium low heat until the onion is translucent. Then add the hot broth, bring to a boil and simmer for 30 to 40 minutes. Strain carefully. Keep hot. When ready to serve, divide the watercress leaves into each soup plate and add the hot broth.

ALMOND BUTTER SMALLMOUTH BASS

¼ cup (approximately 2 oz.) whole almonds
1½ sticks butter unsalted and room temperature
     plus 2-3 tbsp. for cooking the fish
2 tsp. finely chopped parsley
½ tsp. grated orange rind
  Salt and pepper
2 lbs. skinned bass fillets

Make the compound butter 24 hours ahead by placing on a cookie sheet and toasting the almonds in a 300° oven until they turn a pale beige. Remove from oven and cool. When completely cool, put in blender or food processor and blend until they become powder. Whip the butter until soft and fluffy. Add the powdered almonds, parsley, orange zest, and salt and pepper and mix well. Taste for seasoning. Then mound onto plastic wrap. Roll into a cylinder and pop into the freezer. Bring to refrigerator or to room temperature a few hours before serving time. Broil the bass fillets until done, when the meat becomes opaque and lost all translucency. Lace pats of butter on broiled bass and serve.

SAUTÉED TOMATOES

4 large tomatoes, ripe and tasty
2-3 tbsp. good olive oil
    Salt and freshly cracked pepper
    Chopped parsley or thyme

Dip the tomatoes one by one in boiling water. Count to 10 and then dip in ice water. Peel, cut in half, scoop out seeds, remove core, and let drain for 10 minutes. Heat olive oil until water drops sizzle. Add tomatoes cut-side down and cook until juices start evaporating and the bottom browns. Turn and finish. Serve cut-side up, sprinkled with salt and pepper and the parsley and/or thyme.

NOTE: If the tomatoes are too huge, which homegrown ones can be indeed, then cut them in thick slices.

FRIED BREAD

- ½ loaf French bread
- 1 garlic clove halved (optional)
- ½ cup (1 stick) unsalted butter
- Salt and pepper
- 2 tbsp. fontina cheese, grated, or any cheese

Slice the French bread into twelve ½-inch pieces and dry them on a cookie sheet in a 300° oven. Do not let them cook. If you wish, rub one side of the bread with a garlic clove. In a heavy-bottomed sauce pan, melt the stick of butter till it sizzles. Put in the bread and brown both sides. Sprinkle with salt, pepper and cheese and put back in the oven just till the cheese melts.

THE PRETTY EASY DESSERT

There are now several commercial ices or sorbets that are quite nice, my favorites come from Blue Moon Sorbet, such as their Mango Passion. Take 1 or 2 flavors, slightly softened and pack them into a mold, one inside the other and serve with berries or fruit sprinkled with liqueur. For example: raspberries with framboise or peaches with Grand Marnier. Place fruit on the platter around the edge and unmold the ice in the middle. To unmold, cover mold for a few seconds with a hot, wet towel. The ice should just slip out.

Little Fried Perch
Cucumber and Tomato Slices with Basil Vinaigrette
Rosemary New Potatoes

Serves four

There is a difference in potatoes. In general, the smaller, thinner skinned potatoes are sweeter and need less cooking. The bigger and thick skinned potatoes are good for baking. Potatoes should be purchased according to how you plan to cook them, not according to whether you caught the fish in Idaho or Maine.

LITTLE FRIED PERCH

- 2-3 fish per person
- 2-3 cups milk
- Flour for dredging
- 4 tbsp. oil
- Parsley bunches
- Salt and pepper
- Lemon wedges

Gut the small fish with a sharp knife using the point. Wash them. Dry them and soak in a little milk for 10 minutes. Drain. Roll in flour and fry in very hot oil for 4 minutes. Set on paper towels to drain. Fry some bunches of parsley. Drain. Sprinkle fish with fried parsley and salt and pepper. Serve immediately with lemon wedges.

CUCUMBER AND TOMATO SLICES WITH BASIL VINAIGRETTE

- 2 tomatoes washed, peeled and sliced
- 2 cucumbers, washed and sliced
- ½ cup oil
- ½ tsp. prepared mustard
- 2 tbsp. vinegar
- 1 tsp. basil, fresh or revived in a little hot water
- Salt and pepper

After slicing the tomatoes and cukes, arrange attractively on a platter. Now zip the remaining ingredients in the blender. Check the vinaigrette and adjust to suit your taste. Dribble over the tomatoes and cucumbers.

ROSEMARY NEW POTATOES

- 3 new potatoes per person
- 1 tbsp. fresh rosemary
- 2 tbsp. melted butter
- Salt and pepper

Steam or boil the new potatoes for 20 minutes or until soft. Burst the potatoes and sprinkle with rosemary, melted butter, and salt and pepper.

Perch Fillets
Bay Potatoes
Sliced Tomatoes
Fruit

Serves four

PERCH FILLETS

1½ sticks plus 4 tbsp. unsalted butter
4 shallots finely chopped and sautéed till translucent
2 tbsp. tarragon, finely chopped
1 tsp. Worcestershire sauce
Salt and pepper
8-12 perch fillets
Flour for dusting

Whip 1½ sticks of butter till soft and fluffy. Sauté the shallots till translucent. Combine the shallots, whipped butter, tarragon, Worcestershire, and salt and pepper and mix well and season to taste. Mound onto plastic wrap. Shape into a cylinder and freeze 24 hours. Bring to room temperature before using. Dust the perch with flour and sauté hot in the remaining 4 tablespoons of butter. Serve with pats of compound butter on top.

BAY POTATOES

- ½ cup red wine vinegar
- Salt
- 1½ lbs. white boiling potatoes peeled and whole
- ¾ cup olive oil (good quality)
- 3 garlic cloves, medium-sized and coarsely chopped
- 4-5 dried bay leaves
- Balsamic vinegar
- Salt and pepper
- 1½ tbsp. chopped parsley

Bring a large saucepan of water to a boil, add the wine vinegar and some salt. Drop in the potatoes, reduce heat to a simmer and cook until potatoes are done but firm, 30 to 40 minutes. Drain and when cool enough to handle, cut into 1-inch pieces. Heat the olive oil, add the garlic and the bay leaves; bring to a simmer and lower the heat to the lowest heat and cook for 15 to 20 minutes. Remove the bay leaves and discard. Mash the garlic and return it to the warm oil. Pour over the potatoes. Toss, add a little balsamic vinegar, salt and pepper, chopped parsley and toss again.

Red, White, and Green Largemouth Bass
Fried Tomato Slices
Fried Bread
Poached Peaches with Raspberries

Serves four

RED, WHITE, AND GREEN LARGEMOUTH BASS

- 1 small white onion, roughly chopped
- 1 small red onion, roughly chopped
- 1 tbsp. unsalted butter
- 1 fresh green scallion, chopped into ½-inch pieces
- 1 tbsp. parsley, chopped fine
- 2 lbs. fillets
- Olive oil
- Salt and pepper

Sauté the white and red onions in butter until the white is translucent. Add scallion and cook for a few minutes more. Add parsley and stir and set aside. Baste fish with oil and sprinkle with salt and pepper. Broil until golden. Heat onions and season with salt and pepper and serve on top of the fish. Pour any juices from the pan over the fish.

FRIED TOMATO SLICES

4-6 ripe but firm tomatoes (you can use green tomatoes, too.)
1 egg, lightly beaten
Salt and pepper
Pinch of thyme
1 cup fine bread crumbs
4 tbsp. unsalted butter

Slice the tomatoes ½-inch thick. Sprinkle the beaten egg with salt, pepper and a pinch of thyme. Dip each tomato slice first into the egg mixture and then into the bread crumbs. In a heavy skillet melt the butter until sizzling and then add the tomatoes and brown on both sides. Serve at once.

POACHED PEACHES WITH RASPBERRIES

4 cups water
2 cups sugar plus 2 tbsp. for sprinkling
1 tsp. lemon juice
1 vanilla bean, split down the middle
4 perfect peaches, big ones
1 qt. fresh raspberries
Framboise

Slowly bring the water, sugar, lemon juice, and vanilla bean to a boil. Simmer 5 to 10 minutes. Add the peaches unpeeled. Return the syrup to a simmer and let cook about 5 to 8 minutes. Remove peaches to a rack and let cool. Peel when still slightly warm and then chill. Sprinkle the raspberries with a couple tablespoons of sugar and framboise. Let stand for one hour and then add the peaches and serve.

Smallmouth Bass Tempura
White Rice
Sake and Tea
Fortune Cookies

Serves four

You know how to make the rice and you can serve sushi as a first course if you are so inclined.

Choice of vegetables varies with the season.

SPRING LIST: asparagus, zucchini, carrots, broccoli

FALL LIST: sweet potato, zucchini, carrots, broccoli

SMALLMOUTH BASS TEMPURA

    Vegetables (above suggested list)
    Cool water for soaking
1 bottle of vegetable oil
2 egg yolks
1⅔ cups ice water
1⅔ cups sifted flour, plus some for dipping
3-4 lbs. bass, in bite-sized pieces

Cut all the vegetables into stick pieces about ½-inch wide by 2 inches long. If you're using sweet potatoes soak first in some cold water for 15 minutes. Drain, dry and then use. Preheat oil to medium frying temperature, about 340°. Prepare batter. Lightly beat egg yolks. With the ice water in a large bowl, dump the flour in all at once. Stir a few times only. The batter should be gloppy and have the appearance of being only half-mixed. Dip vegetables and fish in flour first. Shake off excess and then mix gently in the batter only to cover and only a few at a time. Fry only a few at a time. Raise temperature slightly for cooking the fish. Let drain on paper towels; serve at once with dipping sauces. A variety of these sauces can be found at many gourmet shops and fancy supermarkets. You will want a soy sauce of some sort; keep to the Japanese types if you can. Mix a little grated ginger with the soy if you like. "Ponzu" is a good soy-type sauce with citrus juices, rice vinegar, malt and wheat.

Panfish on a Stick
Chocolate Chip Cookies

Serves four

This is a nice menu for your young son to have in his daypack when he goes on his first solo outing for fish.

PANFISH ON A STICK

- 4 little panfish, cleaned
- Salt and pepper
- ½ cup corn meal
- 4 tbsp. hot bacon fat

Sprinkle the cleaned fish with salt and pepper. Dip each fish in cornmeal and baste with hot bacon fat. Cook on a stick over the fire until the fish are crispy. If those who volunteered to be stick holders have returned to the fishing hole, you may also pan-fry these fish. After dipping the fish in cornmeal melt 2 tablespoons bacon fat and 2 tablespoons unsalted butter in a pan and fry skin and all.

CHOCOLATE CHIP COOKIES

Use the Nestlé's Toll House cookie recipe and do use salted butter. Add an additional 2 tablespoons of brown sugar (for the 6 oz. size bag of chocolate morsels) to the recipe. Omit nuts. The result is a thin cookie that is crunchy and just a bit chewy.

Basics

Everyone cooks and eats fish. Everyone has an Aunt Lizzie who cooks a mean fish chowder or has a fabulous recipe for flounder or pike or snapper. Eating fish is older than the Bible; everyone knows about it and today—especially with fish now enjoying most-favored and healthy protein status—it is perhaps being eaten and cooked more than ever. There are many, many, many people who know more than I do about how to cook their own particular local fish or their own most frequently caught fish. So how can I be so presumptive, claim expertise, and write a book about cooking fish?

I'm not the absolute authority on the subject of fish cuisine. But I'd like here to add a perspective and culinary skill-set to cooking fish—that of a sport fisherman. Over forty million people hold fresh water fishing licenses, and how many more must there be who fish regularly in the oceans? There are certainly a whole lot of fish being cooked up by sport fishermen. And many of us are not only faced with feeling the requirement to cook what is caught and killed, but that it be cooked with a certain amount of finesse and skill. We feel it in the context of first spending a lot of time fishing and, hopefully, then catching a whole mess of fish.

It is hardest to cook the usual, the common, and the basic. My cooking instructor said one time that a good measure of a cook's true capability is how well she cooks a hamburger. My focus rarely wavers when painting lemon verbena leaves with chocolate to decorate a mold of white chocolate mousse, or when I must figure out a menu using Dall's sheep or porcini mushrooms. But give me my 900th bluefish to cook and, well, it's kinda hard to get excited about it.

Of course, I'd like with this book to change your "usual." Certainly the reason there are so many different cookbooks and that cookbooks sell well every year is because we get a little bored with our usual recipes and simply the variety any new book might offer helps alleviate some of the boredom. But I pass along here a little more than just variety. In thinking through the process of trying to become both a better fisherman and a better cook, I've found that although these two different avocations can certainly get mired in the mundane, it is for that very reason that both also encourage ingenuity. So I'm hoping in addition to introducing you to something new, this book will inspire and lay the groundwork for a more creative approach to cooking fish.

I am very fortunate to have for a number of years spent two weeks fishing in Alaska. Each of the camps we visited had an abundance of Dolly Varden and grayling. (And abundance in Alaska means out and out excess anywhere else.) It would not be uncommon or require much skill, even on a fly, to catch 15 or 20 of either one every day. Yes, this could lead to monotony, and for some it does. They reel the fish in hurriedly, without playing it, and jerking as it comes, hoping rough carelessness will allow the fish to escape, eliminating (wasted) time spent bringing the fish to shore, unhooking, and releasing it. But for many of us the commonness of the little Dolly makes us willing to experiment. Maybe switch to some weird dry fly that the guide invented rather than continue to wave the tried-and-true streamer in front of Ms. Dolly. I heard yesterday someone took a Dolly on a mouse! Let's try it! And with the catching of each fish we learn what makes them alike and familiar and what makes them unique. So many caught one after another makes it easy to begin to recognize its style in the strike, how it fights, and know when it's tired and should be played no longer. But each has its own little personality, too. What, a grayling that jumps and twists when hooked? It must have been taking lessons from a rainbow trout. To know the fish is to respect it. I've had more than one fishing guide who, after the fight and the fish is being released, thanks the fish for the fun it's given us. It is a habit I have found myself imitating. To become engrossed in the fun of experimentation, enjoy familiarity with the fish, to respect it is to learn also how to focus and concentrate on fishing. When three days' fishing seems like lightning fast seconds passing, when the scenes from "The Old Man and the Sea" and Spencer Tracy's monologues with the fish become your reality, then you not only have become a good fisherman but found the ingredients for becoming a good cook.

Cooking is not different from fishing in this respect. The 900th bluefish may taste best grilled, that's fine, but put some zing in your 900th bluefish and try grilling it with a stick of apple wood on the coals or try making the menu more interesting. Serve the grilled bluefish with couscous, not rice, or with porcini, not peas. Taking the time, having the patience, focusing on the preparation is what makes the difference in the success of the meal. If you are willing to do some prep work and to experiment, you'll not only cook better, but have way more fun doing it.

And fishermen do have a head start when it comes to prepping for a good fish dish because they're right there on the water, standing ready to optimize the eating quality of that just-caught fish, taking care of it from the moment it's in the boat, and all just for the sake of having a perfect main course. Try to cool the fish down, eliminate stress—even before it's killed—and keep it cool until it's in the kitchen and about to be cooked. Use the sharpest knives and the greatest care in cleaning the fish. And I've come to learn that having on hand some basic or already prepared ingredients not only makes getting the meal on the table less hectic, but also extends your fishing day without that nagging sense of what am I to serve with this fish dinner? Having some fish accoutrements in the freezer or refrigerator can make the smallmouth bass that suddenly appears for supper that much more exciting. Making a batch of basil compound butter and freezing it just as the basil comes into your garden, or making extra homemade mayonnaise to have around after the chicken salad can make the difference to the serendipitous fish meal.

Just as Mr. Fish has given you the ultimate in fishing and cooking pleasure, it is truly wonderful to be able to pass along some of that pleasure to family or guests. And the bonus is that when you take the ordinary meal and make it really special, your reputation as a very fine cook is secured.

One time when we were in Alaska we heard about a dish that the Inuits prepare in advance and keep on hand for special occasions. It is called "stinky heads." It's prepared in plastic 5-gallon drums which held the previous winter's supply of cooking oil. They gather the heads of all the salmon they can find and when the 5-gallon drum is full they close it up and bury it for a couple of weeks. They know the "stinky heads" are "ready" (dare I say edible) when they can smell the fish odor permeating from the ground. But fear not: "Stinky heads" are not one of my suggestions for keeping about for that spur-of-the-moment fish supper. (As the Inuit woman said, "Stinky heads make your stomach growl.")

Listed in this chapter are just some nice things you should know how to make, have on hand, and have in your brain for making a sudden ooh la la dinner of fish.

RISOTTO

- 4 oz. unsalted butter or a mixture of butter and olive oil
- 1 shallot, chopped very fine
- 1 ½ cups Italian Arborio rice
- 4-5 cups hot chicken stock
- Salt and pepper
- Pinch of saffron threads (optional)
- ¼ cup Parmesan

In a heavy-bottomed, fry pan, heat butter. Sauté the shallot until translucent. Add rice. Cook, stirring until it becomes very white, shiny and very hot to touch. Then, over medium-high heat, add only enough stock so that the rice is just covered. Holding the handle of the pan, firmly swish the rice around and around. Do this every 2 to 3 minutes, keeping a low simmer going in the pot in between. This is so the rice won't stick. (If you weaken and stir the rice, then you must continue to stir until done.) As soon as you can distinguish the grains of rice again, then add another ½ cup of fluid. Keep swirling the pot and adding more fluid as it becomes absorbed. Taste when you feel it is nearly finished. It should be firm to the bite, with a tender, creamy texture—not too dry and not too runny. Season with salt and pepper. If using saffron, dissolve in the hot broth and add halfway through or with the very last addition of the broth. The nearer the end it is added, the stronger the taste. Add Parmesan and serve.

OLIVE BASTING OIL

- 1 cup good olive oil
- 8 peeled garlic cloves
- 1½ tsp. thyme
- 1 bay leaf

Combine and heat on low heat all the ingredients for 20 to 30 minutes. Remove garlic and keep to spread on toast or mash and put in mayonnaise.

MAYONNAISE

¼ cup vinegar or lemon juice
½ tsp. salt
2 tsp. mustard prepared
¼ tsp. ground pepper
1 dash cayenne
3 egg yolks
2 cups good olive oil
1 tbsp. hot water

In a bowl combine: vinegar or lemon juice, salt, mustard, pepper, cayenne. Let salt melt. Add egg yolks. Whisk until frothy and well combined. Add oil very slowly in a dribble until the mayonnaise seems to have started to take and thicken. Then you may add the oil faster. When finished, taste for seasoning and adjust with salt, pepper, mustard, and lemon juice or vinegar. Be sure to dissolve the salt in vinegar or water first as it will not dissolve well in the mayonnaise. Whisk in a tablespoon of hot, hot water to finish it. Any dry herbs added should first be revived in hot water or no flavor will exude through the oil which will coat them. This may also be done in the food processor with no fuss/no mess.

BREAD CRUMBS

You can use either fresh or dried French or Italian bread. If you need to dry the bread further, place slices on cookie sheets in a 300° oven until just hard. Break into pieces and blend in the food processor with the steel blade until fine. Then shake through a strainer. The bread crumbs that result are all of an even size and will give a better texture when cooked.

BASIC VINAIGRETTE

2 tbsp. vinegar
¼ cup good olive oil
1 tsp. prepared mustard
Salt and pepper
Herbs of your choice

Combine all ingredients in a blender and zip on high for a second or two.

Here are some things to buy and keep around:

Fresh herbs—Buy the little plants that come in cheap plastic containers for a few dollars and use the leaves without care or worry to the health of the plant. When the leaves are gone, buy another plant.

Dried wild mushrooms—Most good grocery stores and certainly gourmet shops have them and their earthy taste is much better than the rubbery fresh mushrooms found in grocery stores.

Unsalted butter—Salt is used to mask flavor. We don't want to mask flavor and don't need to add salt to the diet—better to use unsalted butter.

Birdseye Tender Tiny Peas—They are almost as good as the fresh ones and can be used in many dishes.

Pepperidge Farm Pastry Sheets—This is the best store-bought pastry dough. But still will not compare to well-made, homemade pastry. The problem, of course, with homemade pastry is that it's often a bit tricky to handle—and when it doesn't work it really doesn't work. When I was learning pastry in cooking school, one of my discouraged classmates in exasperation left her pastry "homework"—a small grey disk of tough dough—at the teacher's doorstep, rang the bell and bolted. No one ever 'fessed up to the sad attempt at pastry, but we had our suspicions—and sympathized. It's hard to make!

Over the years I have learned a few tricks and have come also to rely on my favorite chef, and cookbook writer of all time, Alice Waters, for good pastry recipes. I am especially fond of the galette dough, which she says came originally from Jacques Pépin. It isn't as elegant as her puff pastry—but it does have almost as much butter and is nearly foolproof to make.

So here is Jacques'/Alice's recipe now with some of my small additions for producing, well, a reliably good tart:

GALETTE DOUGH

- 2 cups unbleached, all-purpose flour
- 1 tsp. sugar
- ¼ tsp. salt
- 12 tbsp. unsalted butter (1½ sticks), chilled and cut into ½-inch pieces
- 7 tbsp. ice water

In the bowl of a standing mix master, fitted with a pastry blender (not the whisk attachment) combine the flour, sugar, and salt. Add in 4 tablespoons of the cold butter slices and mix until the flour mixture resembles course cornmeal. Then add in the remaining stick of butter slices and blend just until the biggest pieces of butter look like large peas—or a bit larger. Remove the bowl from the mixer and bit by bit—a tablespoonful at a time—add the cold water. After each addition of water toss the mixture, letting it fall through your fingers. Try not to squeeze the dough together or you'll overwork it, making it tough. Keep tossing the dough until it begins to look ropey and is coming together. It will have some dry patches, and if there are more dry patches than rope, add more water. Lay two big pieces of plastic wrap on the counter and form the dough into two rough balls. Place each ball on a piece of the plastic wrap and fold the wrap over the ball, pushing the dough together, and then flattening it into a 4-inch disk. Refrigerate for at least 30 minutes before rolling out. (The dough disk can also be frozen at this point for a few weeks.)

Working with one of the dough disks at a time, take it from the fridge and let it soften. In the meantime, cut a large piece of parchment paper, big enough to accommodate a 14-inch round of pastry dough, and dust it lightly with flour. When the dough has softened remove the wrap and place the disk on the parchment. Flour the top lightly and pinch the edges of the dough so there are no cracks. Now place two sheets of plastic wrap, overlapping, over the dough and roll it out, pressing as you go at first, then just rolling it to about a 14-inch circle and an ⅛ of an inch or less thick. Slide the dough/parchment paper onto the back side of a big cookie sheet and put in the refrigerator for about a half hour or more before using. Each disk is enough for one open tart.

Good cooking oils—A good, green olive oil, a walnut or a hazelnut oil are good oils and can be purchased through catalogs, gourmet shops, and good grocery stores. The walnut oil and hazelnut oils will go rancid if you don't use them up after five months or so. Since it is expensive it might be worth finding a friend to split a bottle with.

Sun-dried tomatoes— These are so wonderful and have so many uses, they're worth having on hand throughout the year. They can be found—both the dried version and then packed in oil (much pricier) now in grocery stores as well as gourmet shops.

Interesting liqueurs and brandy—They will turn a dull item into something very interesting and are fun to play with.

Breads—Having homemade herb bread around can do the same as the homemade jellies—really add class to the meal. Squishy white bread does not seem to have the same effect.

Compound butter—Several different compound butters are listed in this book and all can be kept in the freezer for at least a couple weeks. They are good for those last-minute attempts at making a dinner ooh la la. Also provides a good vehicle for freezing some of the hard-to-get fresh herbs.

Good sharp knives—A good set of very sharp knives sounds like suggesting you need a pepper grinder—rather obvious. But I cannot overemphasize how much more pleasant working on fish can be, if done with a variety of sizes of sharp knives that are well suited to your hand. When John Hewitt came to visit his house present was to sharpen my knives and no better present could there be.

Parchment paper and plastic wrap— Both of these items you likely have on hand anyway, but are very useful for all the breads and pastry-making included in this book. I use the plastic wrap to cover pastry when I roll it out—don't have to smother it in flour that way—to prevent sticking. And I also use the parchment paper (lightly floured) for pastry to prevent sticking and also if it is free-standing and doesn't go in a dish, just on a pizza stone to cook; likewise for breads.

Pasta Machines—If you like making your own pasta, a hand-crank machine that kneads and cuts it is indispensible. Also available now are attachments for a Kitchen Aid standing mixer that produce all sorts of different shaped pasta. It's an expensive item but requires less effort, time over the hand-crank version, plus produces a variety of fun shapes.

HOMEMADE PASTA

  1½ cups semolina
    2 eggs
        All-purpose flour for dusting
        Salt
        Couple of drops of olive oil for the boiling water
    2 tbsp. unsalted butter, melted

Make a mountain of the semolina on the counter-top and then make a crater in the mountain. Lightly beat the eggs together and pour into the crater. With a fork bring the semolina into the egg mixture slowly until all the semolina is moist, then form into two small balls. If the dough is at all sticky, add more semolina—the dough needs to be very dry. Knead for 10-20 minutes and then shape into two 8-inch long (or so) snakes. Cut each snake into 6 pieces. Take one of the pieces and knead it for a few minutes. Flatten with the palm of your hand until it is thin enough to crank through the pasta machine on the widest setting (#1). Fold the pasta and crank through again. Repeat this two more times on this setting. Now put the pasta sheet through each progressively higher setting on the machine without folding it until the pasta sheet is the desired thickness. For me, this is usually after the second to the last setting (#5). Finally cut the pasta and lay on a floured cutting board and sprinkle with all-purpose flour. Toss pasta with your fingers so it is well dusted with the flour. Repeat the procedure for the remaining pieces of dough. The pasta may now be left to dry.

Of course dried pasta can be stored or cooked immediately. Fresh pasta cooks very quickly in boiling water—be sure to add salt to the water and a drop of oil—only about 2 to 3 minutes.

If you are trying to think of a good salad to have with your fish, here are several which might suit your meal, or at least spark an idea.

GREEN AND PURPLE COLE SLAW

- 3 cups finely shredded green Savoy cabbage
- 3 cups finely shredded purple cabbage
- 1 large carrot, grated
- ½ tsp. salt
- 2 tsp. prepared mustard
- ¼ tsp. ground pepper
- 1 dash cayenne
- 3 egg yolks
- 2 cups corn oil or good olive oil
- 1 tsp. salt
- ¼ cup vinegar
- 2 tsp. sugar
- ¼ cup sour cream
- 2 tsp. lemon juice
- 2 tsp. caraway seeds
- 1 tbsp. dry mustard

Keep the cabbages separate. Divide the carrot between them.

Now make a mayonnaise by combining in a bowl: ½ teaspoon salt, the prepared mustard, pepper, and cayenne. Let the salt melt and add the egg yolks. Whisk until frothy and well combined. Add the oil slowly in a dribble, whisking all the while, until the mayonnaise begins to thicken. Then you may add the oil faster. When finished, taste for seasoning and adjust. Add a tablespoon of hot water to finish it off. This also can be made in a food processor. Now add the remaining 7 ingredients—making sure to dissolve the salt in the vinegar first to better dissolve it—to the mayonnaise and divide between the two cabbages. Mix well and taste for seasoning. You will want a nice sweet sour taste. Grate a little black pepper over each and chill for several hours. Mix again before serving a heaping spoonful of each color of dressed cabbage per plate.

PANZANELLA SALAD

- 8 thick slices day-old Italian or French bread
- ½ cup chicken stock
- 3 tbsp. butter
- 2 tomatoes, peeled, seeded, and coarsely chopped
- 1 medium cucumber, seeded and chopped
- 1 small red onion, chopped
- 1 head romaine lettuce
- A few bitter greens, such as chicory or escarole
- Shredded fresh basil leaves
- A good vinaigrette—your own, or see page 217
- Salt and pepper

Cut the bread into large cubes and dribble the stock over the cubes and toss. Fry in butter until crisp and let cool. Combine all remaining ingredients and toss with the vinaigrette. Check for salt and pepper and let sit a little to meld the flavors. Add croutons and toss and serve.

EGG AND ASPARAGUS SALAD

2 hard-boiled eggs
1 tbsp. white vinegar
½ lb. asparagus, peeled
2 heads Boston lettuce, cleaned and dried
1 tbsp. balsamic vinegar
1 tsp. prepared mustard
¼ cup olive oil
   Salt and pepper
1 tbsp. mayonnaise

To hard-boil the eggs, set in cold water with a tablespoon of white vinegar, bring to a boil, reduce to a medium simmer and cook, using a timer, for 9 minutes. Then plunge in cold water. Peel, chop and set aside.

Steam the asparagus, cut into 1-inch pieces and combine with the lettuce. Make a vinaigrette by combining in the blender the balsamic vinegar, mustard, oil and dashes of salt and pepper and blending for a second or two. Add the mayonnaise and motorize for another second. Toss the vinaigrette first with the asparagus and lettuce and then add chopped egg. Toss lightly, taste for salt and pepper and serve.

CHICORY SALAD

- 1 small head chicory
- 1 head Boston lettuce
- 1 small bunch watercress
- 6 slices medium crisp bacon, or better yet, pancetta

For the dressing:

- 3 tbsp. vinegar
- Salt and pepper
- 1 tsp. prepared mustard
- 1 tsp. tarragon, revived in a little hot water
- 1 very small clove garlic, mashed and then chopped very fine
- ¼ cup olive oil

Wash the greens carefully. Shake dry and roll up in clean terry towels. (This can be done several hours before using.) Combine all the ingredients for the dressing in a blender and blend on high. Toss salad with dressing. Add bacon or pancetta and then taste and adjust seasoning.

SALAD OF ZUCCHINI AND YELLOW SQUASH AND TOMATO

- ¼ tsp. each of salt and pepper
- 2 tbsp. good vinegar
- ⅓ cup olive oil
- 1 tsp. good prepared mustard
- Fresh basil leaves—the little-leafed kind, if possible, called spicy globe
- 2 tiny zucchini, julienned
- 3 tiny yellow squash, julienned
- Corn oil or cooking oil
- 1 head Boston lettuce or 2 Bibb, cleaned
- 1 tomato, skinned, seeded, drained and julienned

First mix salt and pepper and vinegar and then add the olive oil, mustard, and basil leaves and zip in the blender for a second or two. Sauté zucchini and yellow squash in corn oil until they just begin to cook. Be sure they keep some of their crispness. Let cool. Toss with lettuce, tomatoes and dressing, or you can keep the squashes separate and lay the alternate colors out in groups on top of the lettuce. Taste for salt and pepper.

WATERCRESS SALAD

- 1 garlic clove, peeled and crushed
- 2 tbsp. wine vinegar
- 1 tsp. prepared mustard
- 1 tsp. soy sauce
- Salt and pepper
- ⅓ cup good quality olive oil
- Bunch watercress without stems, washed
- 2 heads Bibb or 1 head Boston lettuce, washed
- ½ head red lettuce, washed

Rub salad bowl with garlic. Combine in the blender the vinegar, mustard, soy sauce, and salt and pepper and zip on high for a second or two. Add olive oil and blend again. Toss with the greens and serve.

THREE GREEN SALAD

3 tbsp. wine vinegar
Salt and pepper
2 tsp. good prepared mustard
¼ tsp. garlic, chopped fine or squeezed through a press
A dash of soy sauce
½ cup olive oil
1 tbsp. mayonnaise
At least three different greens; endive, watercress, Boston lettuce or whatever is available to you
6 strips of cooked bacon

Combine the vinegar, salt and pepper, mustard, garlic and soy sauce. Add the oil and mix well. Now add the mayonnaise and mix well again. Toss dressing with the greens. Crumble the bacon into the salad and toss again.

CHICORY AND ESCAROLE SALAD

1 tbsp. vinegar
Salt and pepper
1 small shallot
1 very small garlic clove, chopped extra fine
⅓ cup light olive oil
1 tbsp. heavy cream
Grated rind of 1 orange
1 head Boston lettuce, washed and dried
1 small head escarole, washed and dried
1 small head chicory, washed and dried
1 orange in sections and cleaned of membranes

Combine vinegar, salt and pepper, shallot, and garlic. Let stand a bit to dissolve salt, then add oil, cream and orange rind. Mix well. Toss with lettuces and orange segments.

SALAD OF MELON, PEARS, AND CUCUMBERS

- 2 tbsp. red wine vinegar
- 1 tsp. mustard
- ½ cup hazelnut or walnut oil
- Salt and pepper
- ½ cup hazelnuts, toasted and chopped coarsely
- 4 pears
- Lemon juice
- 1 small melon
- 2 medium sized cucumbers
- Lettuce

Combine the vinegar, mustard, oil and salt and pepper in the blender. Turn on high for a couple of seconds and then set aside. Toast the hazelnuts in the oven set at 300°. Remove and cover with a towel for 5 or 10 minutes, then rub off the skins and chop coarsely. Peel, core, and slice the pears and toss with a little lemon juice. Add slices of melon, about an equal amount to the pears. Peel, seed, and slice the cucumbers. Toss the cucumbers, pears and melon together with the vinaigrette and let sit an hour or so. Just before serving toss in the toasted hazelnuts and serve on a bed of lettuce.

BIBB SALAD

- 2 tbsp. red wine vinegar
- ½ cup good olive oil
- 1 tsp. prepared mustard
- Salt and pepper
- 4 heads Bibb lettuce, cleaned
- A few snips of chive

Combine vinegar, oil, mustard, and salt and pepper in a blender and zip on high for a second or two. Toss with the lettuce and chives.

GREEN SALAD

- 1 tbsp. vinegar
- 1 tsp. prepared mustard
- ½ cup oil
- 1 tsp. basil
- Salt and pepper
- Head of Boston, red, oak leaf, or Bibb lettuce (no strong tastes)

Blend all but the lettuce in the blender on high-speed. Toss with the lettuce.

CUCUMBER AND TOMATO SLICES WITH BASIL VINAIGRETTE

- 2 tomatoes washed, peeled and sliced
- 2 cucumbers, washed and sliced
- ½ cup oil
- ½ tsp. prepared mustard
- 2 tbsp. vinegar
- 1 tsp. basil, fresh or revived in a little hot water
- Salt and pepper

After slicing the tomatoes and cukes, arrange attractively on a platter. Now zip the remaining ingredients in the blender. Check the vinaigrette and adjust to suit your taste. Dribble over the tomatoes and cucumbers.

Index

Apples, Baked, 141, 143
Apricot, 92, 94, 170, 172
Artichoke Hearts, 36, 37, 60, 62, 74
Artichokes, 92, 93
Asparagus, 58, 59

Banana Chips, 95, 102
Basics, 213
Bass, Freshwater, 199
   Largemouth, Red, White, and Green, 208
   Smallmouth, Almond Butter, 201, 202
   Smallmouth, Tempura, 210
Bass, Black Sea, Chinese Style, 128, 129
Bass, Sea, Grilled with Sun-Dried Tomatoes, Pepper and Garlic, 122, 123
Bass, Striped
   Broiled with Wild Mushrooms and Tomato, 60, 61
Beans
   Fava with Asparagus, 160, 161
   Green, 98, 99
Birdseye Tender Tiny Peas, 218
Blancmange, 179, 180
Blueberries, 81, 83
   with Crème Anglaise, 81, 83
Bluefish
   Broiled with Thyme and Noisette Butter, 58
   Grilled, 51, 55, 56, 71, 74
   with Lime Mayonnaise, 64
Bread
   corn, 109, 110, 154, 155
   crumbs, 217
   French Whole Wheat, 46
   Fried, 116, 117, 118, 126, 127, 201, 203, 208
   Sage, 39, 40
   Tomato, 144, 145
Broccoli, Fried, 46, 47
Brownies, 48, 49, 159, 165, 166
Butter
   Anchovy Garlic, 144, 145
   Black Olive and Basil, 32, 33
   Noisette, 190, 191
   Roasted Red Pepper, 87
   Unsalted, 218

Cabbage, 183, 185
Cake
   Chocolate, 68, 70
   Sponge, 156, 158
   Straw Potato-Corn, 122, 124
Cantaloupe Ice, 55, 57
Carrots, Julienned, 32, 34
Catfish, 189
   Fried, 194
   The Best, 192, 193
Char
   Grilled with Tarragon and Shallot Butter, 165
   Leftover Risotto, 170
Chocolate Roll, 60, 63
Chowder
   Corn, 92
   Fish, 120
Cole Slaw, 87, 88
   Green and Purple, 222
Consommé, Chicken, 201
Cookies
   Almond, 167, 169
   Chocolate Chip, 211
   Fortune, 79, 114, 115, 128
   Sugar, 32, 35, 58, 59, 107
Cool Vegetables with Herb Mayonnaise, 177, 178
Cornbread, 109, 110, 154, 155
Couscous, 177, 179
   with Wild Mushrooms and Chives, 66
Crab
   Cakes with Sherry and Garlic Mayonnaise, 146, 147
   Szechwan for Sunday Night Supper, 150
Crème Anglaise, 74, 76, 81, 83, 160, 162
Crème Brulée, Apricot, 170, 172
Cucumber and Tomato Slices with Basil Vinaigrette, 204, 205
Cucumbers, Sautéed, 163, 164

Dessert, The Pretty Easy, 201, 203
Dolphin, Capered, 100
Dough, Galette, 218, 219

Fiddleheads, 32, 34

Figs, 32, 34, 35
Flan, Wild Mushroom and Potato, 186, 187
Flounder
  and Scallop Soup, 118
  Chinese Grilled with Noodles, 114
  Gray, 116
Franey, Pierre, 18
Freshwater Fish, 151

Grand Marnier, 25, 28, 29, 31, 43, 45
Grayling, Pan Poached, 167
Grits, 133, 134, 194, 195

Herbs, Fresh, 218
Honeydew, 181, 182

Ice Cream
  Coconut, 109, 111
  Honey, 125
Ice
  Apricot, 92, 94
  Cantaloupe, 55, 57
  Honeydew, 181, 182

Kingfish with Lime Butter, 95
Knowles, 131

Labrador, 23
Lobster with Anchovy Garlic Butter, 144

Mackerel
  Grilled Lemon-Thyme, 71
  Grilled Mackerel, 74
Mayonnaise, 217
  Green, 25, 26
  Herb, 177, 178
  Lime, 64
  Sherry and Garlic, 146, 147, 148
Melon, 79, 84, 86
  Drunk, 144, 145
Mozzarella, 36

Mushrooms
  Dried wild, 218
  wild, 60

Mussels
  Pizza, 138
  Steamed, 136

Oil
  Olive Basting, 216
  Good cooking, 220
Orange Jelly, 66, 67
Orange Oranges, 173, 174
Oyster Stew, 133

Panfish, 199
  on a Stick, 211
Parchment paper, 220
Parmesan Rolls, 170, 171
Parsley, Fried, 190, 191
Pasta
  Fried with Water Chestnuts, 84
  Homade, 221
  Machines, 220
  with Fresh Corn and Basil, 165
  with Parmesan and Romano Cheeses, 181, 182
  with Spinach and Artichoke Hearts, 74
Pastry, Sweet with Jam, 100, 101
Pea Pods, Stir Fried, 150
Peaches, Poached with Raspberries, 208, 209
Pears, 32, 34, 35
Peas, 36, 37, 60, 62, 64, 65
  and Artichoke Hearts, 36, 37, 60, 62
  Snow, 64, 65
    Stir-fry with Broccoli, 128
Pépin, Jacques, 218
Pepperidge Farm Pastry Sheets, 218
Perch
  Fillets, 206
  Little Fried, 204
Persimmons, Broiled, 194, 195
Pike, 175
  Couscous, 177
Piña Coladas, 102

Pineapple
  Grilled, 177, 178
  Grilled with Orange Ice, 102, 103
  Grilled with Strawberries, 190, 191
Pizza, 81, 82, 138, 139
Poached Pears and Figs, 32, 34
Polenta, Grilled, 55, 56
Pompano, Grilled with Mint and Orange Rind, 107
Popovers, 43, 44
  Summer, 43, 44
  Summer II, 74
Potato
  Bay, 206, 207
  Boiled New, 64, 65
  Cake, 95, 96
  Flan, 68, 69
  Gratin, 29, 30
  Grilled Idaho, 87, 88
  New, Dilled, 163, 164
  New, Rosemary, 204, 205
  Pink New Boiled, 196, 197
  Sautéed with Chanterelles and Thyme, 167, 168
Pudding, Grand Marnier Rice, 25, 28

Quebec, 23

Raspberries, 59, 63, 74, 76
  with Crème Anglaise, 74, 76
Raspberry Ice, 58, 59
Redfish, 51, 68
Rhubarb Fool, 196, 198
Rice
  Brown with Pignoli Nuts and Green Beans, 107, 108
  Pilaf, 36, 37
  White, 98, 102, 128
Risotto, 216

Salad
  Bibb, 109, 110, 228
  Bibb Lettuce and Bittergreens, 68
  Cabbage Patch Pasta, 183, 185
  Caesar, 136, 138, 140
  Chicory, 146, 149, 225
  Chicory and Escarole, 55, 56, 227
  Cucumber and Tomato Slices with Basil Vinaigrette, 229
  Egg and Asparagus, 141, 142, 224
  Green, 229
  Green with Oil and Vinegar, 181
  Melon, Pears and Cucumbers, 84, 228
  Nice Green, 66, 71, 81
  Panzanella, 90, 223
  Red, Green and Yellow Pepper, 100
  Sherbet, Strawberry, 90, 91
  Three Green, 39, 42, 227
  Watercress, 26, 27, 29, 30, 42, 226
  Your Nice Green, 66, 107, 122
  Zucchini and Yellow Squash and Tomato, 25, 27
  Zucchini, yellow squash and tomato, 226
Salmon
  Atlantic, 23, 39
  Calzone, 48
  Chapter, 23
  coho, 39
  Grilled Whole, 36
  Hash Patties, 39, 40
  Medallions, 32, 33
  Medallions with Black Olive and Basil Butter, 32
  Pacific, 23, 39
  Pacific compared to Atlantic, 39
  Salad, 27, 29, 30, 39, 42, 43, 46, 48
  Scallops, 29
  Smoked Salmon Salad, 46
  Steaks, 32
  Whole Poached, 25, 26
Saltwater Fish
  Bottom, 113
  Chapter on, 51
  Inshore, 53
  Offshore, 77
Sauterne, 107
Shad, 189
  Roe, 196, 197
Shallots, 179, 181, 183, 184
Shark, Mako
  Steaks with Lemon Dill, 98
Shellfish, 131
Shrimp
  Gratin, 137
  Little, 141, 142

Smelt, 189
   Fried with Noisette Butter, 190
Snapper, Red, Grilled with Lime Butter Sauce and Grilled Pineapple, 109
Sorbet, Pear, 114, 115

Soufflé, Grand Marnier, 31, 45
   Another, 30, 35, 38, 41, 43, 45
Soup
   Rice and Parsley, 98
   Sorrel, 196
Spinach, Sautéed, 116, 117
Sponge, Strawberry, 156, 158
Squash, Broccoli, and Turnips in Wine, 173
Steelhead, 160
Strawberries, 158, 160, 162
Stream Fish, 153
Swordfish
   Grilled Steaks, 92, 93
   Grilled with Garlic Butter, 90
   Grilled with Roasted Red Pepper Butter, 87

Tart
   Apple, 135
   Fig, 118, 119
   Raspberry, 36, 38
   Tomato and Eggplant, 71, 72
Tautog with Asparagus and Vegetables, 126, 127
Tomato
   Fried Slices, 208, 209
Tomatoes
   Broiled, 179
   Cherry, Sautéed, 165, 166
   Perfect with Cognac Dressing, 58, 59
   Sautéed, 201, 202
   Stuffed Risotto, 156
   Sun-dried, 220
Trifle, Summer, 87, 89
Trout
   Breakfast, 154
   Fried, 156
   Poached Steelhead with Lemon Butter Sauce, 160
   Streamside with Potatoes, 159
   with Noisette Butter, 163

Tuna
   Grilled with Lemon Butter, 84, 85
   Japanese Leftover, 79, 80
   Steaks, 81
Tuttifrutti, Real, 95, 97

Vinaigrette
   Basic, 217
   Basil, 204, 205

Wahoo Steaks Shish Kebab, 102
Walleye, 175
   en Papillotte, 181
   Lemon-Lime, 186
   Sautéed with Noisette Butter and Shallots, 179
   Steaks with Béarnaise Sauce, 183
Walleye and Pike, 175
Watercress, Sautéed, 79, 80, 114, 115
Waters, Alice, 218
Weakfish
   Broiled with Mint and Garlic, 66
Whitefish, Steamed, 173

Zucchini, 156, 158

About the author:

REBECCA GRAY has written eleven books about food, including the best-selling *Eat Like a Wild Man* and this book's companion, *The New Gray's Wild Game Cookbook*. She has been a contributing editor for *Sports Afield* and *Attaché* and written for *Field & Stream*, *SAVEUR*, *Town & Country*, *Playboy*, *Outside*, *Martha Stewart Living*, and many other publications. Most recently she served as an expert editor for the 75th anniversary edition of the *Joy of Cooking*. With her husband, Ed Gray, she founded *Gray's Sporting Journal*, the prestigious magazine about hunting and fishing. She lives in Lyme, New Hampshire.

www.ingramcontent.com/pod-product-compliance
Lightning Source LLC
Chambersburg PA
CBHW031243290426
44109CB00012B/413